JOY

in the

New Testament

William G. Morrice

WILLIAM B. EERDMANS PUBLISHING COMPANY
GRAND RAPIDS, MICHIGAN

First published 1984 by The Paternoster Press, England
This edition published 1985 through special arrangement with
Paternoster by Wm. B. Eerdmans Publishing Company,
255 Jefferson S.E., Grand Rapids, Mich. 49503

Library of Congress Cataloging in Publication Data

Morrice, William G.
JOY IN THE NEW TESTAMENT

Includes index.
1. Joy — Biblical teaching. 2. Bible. N.T.
— Criticism, interpretation, etc. I. Title.
BS2545.J6M67 1985   241′.4   85-1632

ISBN 0-8028-0071-8

CONTENTS

To Katharine

FOREWORD

I count it a privilege to be asked to write a foreword to this fine study of 'Joy in the New Testament' from the pen of one of my most distinguished students in Aberdeen University.

'Man's chief end', says the Shorter Catechism, 'is to glorify God and enjoy him for ever.' In the past we have had learned studies on Faith (*pistis*) and Love (*agapē*), but, to my knowledge, none, or few, on Joy (*chara*). Dr Morrice's book, the fruit of long study of the various words for Joy in the New Testament, fills the lacuna.

It begins with the great need for 'joy' in that pessimistic world of the Stoics to which the Good News of the Gospel came, and goes on to study the various New Testament words for that 'conquering new-born joy' which (in Matthew Arnold's words) broke on the world with the birth of Jesus Christ and 'filled her life with day'.

Then, one by one, Dr Morrice goes on to study the various nouns and verbs used in the New Testament to express the optimism and gladness which were the fruits of belief in the 'Good News' which apostles like Paul and Peter proclaimed to the men and women of the first century A.D.

Today, when we live in a world when men's hearts again fail them for fear of what may be in store for mankind, Dr Morrice's book is a rousing recall of that radiant optimism which began with the coming of Christ and which fills the pages of the New Testament from the four Gospels to the Revelation of St John the Divine.

A. M. HUNTER

PREFACE

This book is a revised edition of the first two sections of a Ph.D. thesis submitted several years ago to the University of Aberdeen. The third section was published in a popularized form as *We Joy in God* by S.P.C.K. in February, 1977.

My thanks are due to Professor A. M. Hunter, formerly of the Chair of Biblical Criticism at Aberdeen University and Master of Christ's College, Aberdeen. Not only did he suggest to me the subject of the Christian conception of joy according to the New Testament and supervise my research into it. He has also gone the second mile by graciously agreeing to write a Foreword to this present volume.

I wish to express thanks also to the Rev. W. B. R. Macmillan, Minister of St. Mary's Church, Dundee, for reading the whole manuscript at an earlier stage of its development and for making valuable comments.

Unless otherwise stated, biblical quotations, including those from the Apocrypha, are taken from the New English Bible.

Finally, I dedicate this book to my wife as a present in this year of our silver wedding.

Cranmer Hall,
Durham.   WM G. MORRICE

INTRODUCTION

SUCH NEED OF JOY

The ancient world at the time of the birth of Jesus Christ was sorely in need of a Saviour. Gone, for the most part, were the old beliefs in the pagan gods and nothing had arisen to take their place. There were many attempts to find the truth and to express it in terms that would satisfy the quest of the human heart for God. Eventually, out of the conflict of religions in the early Roman Empire, Christianity emerged as the victor over its pagan rivals. It owed its triumph not to any similarities between it and other faiths, but to its uniqueness and to its inherent superiority over them all.

The desperate need felt by the pre-Christian era showed itself in the development of certain philosophical and religious movements within the pagan world itself. Chief of these were Stoicism, Epicureanism, and the mystery religions.

Stoicism

It is generally recognised that it was in Stoicism that the mind of antiquity reached its highest peak of expression. Not only so, but that expression had become popular in a way unparalleled in previous history since "the Stoic missionary, preaching the self-sufficiency of virtue in a threadbare cloak at the street-corners, had been one of the typical figures of a Greek town for many generations before St. Paul".[1]

Founded by Zeno about 315 B.C. and later expanded and systematised by Chrysippus of Soli, Stoicism taught that the chief end of man was happiness and that this was to be won by acting in conformity with nature. This happiness of the virtuous man, however, was more negative than positive since it consisted in independence from external circumstances and in the peace of mind obtained by moral conduct. Through philosophy, the Stoic could live without fear and rise superior to the troubles of life.

The Stoic school continued to flourish until it became the religion of the early Roman Empire. It even enunciated some sort of doctrine of immortality with the thought of a future life of bliss. Yet Stoicism was a stern creed at best and often caused its adherents to fall into despair. Lofty as was its teaching in many respects, it was mainly concerned with the training of people to endure evil in the world. There was no joy in it. Stoicism was essentially pessimistic in spirit, and its outlook upon life was dark and foreboding.

Epicureanism

Epicurus, a contemporary of Zeno, saw the secret of happiness in the enjoyment of simple pleasures and in freedom from troublous thoughts—especially those connected with religion. Lucretius gave poetic expression to Epicureanism in his *De Rerum Natura*, stating as his purpose the attempt to deliver men from bondage to religion and from fear of death. He maintained that the gods dwell apart in eternal peace, far removed from earthly trials and turmoils, and quite indifferent to the troubles and sorrows of mankind.

According to Epicurus and his followers, there was no place at all in religion for joy—except in the case of the gods themselves, who lived a life of perpetual happiness and bliss. The self-appointed task of the philosopher was to free men from the terrors and degradations of religion. He tried to do so by giving a popular and rational exposition of the origin and nature of the universe without resorting to the hypothesis of supernatural agencies.

The Mystery Religions

The most celebrated of the mystery religions were the Eleusinian, the Orphic and the Dionysiac Mysteries. The main characteristic of the orgiastic cult of Dionysus was the ecstasy or enthusiasm manifested in wild revels by torchlight on the mountain side, accompanied by tumultuous music. The Orphic sects followed the Dionysiac ritual closely, but they liberated it from its savage excesses. The highest and finest expression of Greek popular religion was to be found in the Eleusinian Mysteries. Yet our knowledge of them is very scanty on account of the fact that the silence imposed upon those initiated into them has been well kept.

One and all, the mystery religions tried to satisfy the intense longing felt by men and women for union and reconciliation with the divine. The Greeks considered that only the gods could be completely happy and that human beings could share in this blissful state only by means of mystic cults of initiation, whereby union with the deity was attained. The mystery religions thus provide us with "another indication of the pathetic yearning of the ancient world for regeneration and salvation".[2]

The Hebrew Race and the Ancient World

When we turn to the Hebrew race, we find there also an intense longing for salvation. Even among the Jews, the dominant note was one of gloom for the world as a whole. Their only hope lay in Yahweh, whom they expected to intervene in history to set things right for themselves as a nation. Thus in the apocalyptic writings there is visible a certain pessimism with regard to this world and all its affairs.

Maurice Jones sums up the situation in the ancient world: "It was a world where the burden of sin and of human misery was intensely realised, and at no period of his history did man express more clearly his need of redemption."[3]

Mommsen opens the closing paragraph of his *History of Rome* with these words: "We have reached the end of the Roman Republic. ... There was in the world as Caesar found it much of the noble heritage of past centuries and an infinite abundance of pomp and glory, but little spirit, still less taste, and least of all true delight in life. It was an old world; and even

the richly-gifted patriotism of Caesar could not make it young
again. The dawn does not return till after the night has fully set
in and run its course. ..."[4]

Into this old world came "good tidings of great joy" (Lk.
2:10); and what Caesar could not do, what the Stoics, the
Epicureans, and the mystery religions had all failed to do, Jesus
Christ did. There came into the world with his birth a new spirit
that changed all things and gave to men and women the possibility of victory over fear and dejection. "After Jesus lived and
died in it, the world was never the same again. A new and unknown spiritual energy entered into the process of human life."[5]
The joy that was one of the main characteristics of the new faith
eventually swept over the world and captured it for Christ.

A Conquering, New-born Joy

Matthew Arnold has given expression to this great truth in
Obermann Once More[6] —written in honour of Senacour, a little-
known French author whose principal composition, *Obermann,*
attracted Matthew Arnold. In this poem, Arnold tells of an
imaginary conversation with Senacour, who, in the following
lines, is supposed to be talking to the poet:

> On that hard pagan world disgust
>   And secret loathing fell.
> Deep weariness and sated lust
>   Made human life a hell.

Then there comes a description of the fast life led by the Roman
noble. In contrast to the West, however, the "brooding East"
discovered the true secret of joy—"a conquering, new-born joy
awoke, and filled her life with day"—and pointed it out to the
West; whose life was thereby changed.

> And centuries came and ran their course,
>   And unspent all that time.
> Still, still went forth that Child's dear force,
>   And still was at its prime.

The poem proceeds to put into the mouth of the author of
Obermann the thought that, with the fading of belief in Christ

in recent years, the storm of unbelief swept over Europe and "in ruins fell the worn-out world we knew". To this broken world, the following words of rebuke are addressed:

> Your creeds are dead, your rites are dead,
>   Your social order too!
> Where tarries he, the Power who said:
>   "See, I make all things new"?
> And yet men have such need of joy!
>   But joy whose grounds are true;
> And joy that should all hearts employ
>   As when the past was new.

The French author explains to Matthew Arnold that it was for that reason that he fled to the wilderness and to seclusion. His last word to the poet is one of encouragement to him to persevere in speaking the message of hope and joy to the world.

> What still of strength is left, employ,
>   This end to help attain:
> One common wave of thought and joy
>   Lifting mankind again!

Such was the message and commission of Senacour to Matthew Arnold. The purpose of this book is to show that the basis of the Christian conception of joy is not out of date. The New Testament is the most joyful book in the world. In Part One, we examine in turn various groups of Greek words for joy. These words occur a total of 326 times in the New Testament. In Part Two, we study the joy of Jesus and then each of the New Testament writers from the point of view of joy. We shall discover that, almost without exception, each has his own contribution to make to this important concept.

As I have tried to show elsewhere[7], this idea is firmly rooted in New Testament theology. It is an essential element in the Christian faith when this is rightly understood. Present-day Christians must be recalled to what Matthew Arnold has called that "conquering, new-born joy" that broke into the world with the birth of Jesus Christ and "filled her life with day".

Part One
VARIETIES OF JOY

1

EXULTANT JOY
agallian, agalliasis

Classical Greek and Septuagint

Two short word pictures chosen from many examples in classical Greek may serve to illustrate the origin of *exultant joy*. The first is from Homer. Odysseus talks to the goddess Calypso of "swift sailing-ships *rejoicing* in the breeze" (*Odyssey* 5.157). The second picture comes from Euripides' *Bacchae* (157), where the ecstatic devotees of the god "sing praise of Dionysus to the beat of the rumbling drums, in joy *glorifying* the lord of joy with Phrygian crying and calling".

The verb (*agallein*) is frequently found in Pindar, Aristophanes and Plato. It is used especially of paying honour to a god.

When we turn to the Septuagint, it is to discover that a new verb has been formed from the same root (*agallian*). It seems that it was felt necessary to form a new word. None of the phrases used in profane or secular Greek was adequate to express joy in Yahweh, the Hebrew God of salvation.[1] Furthermore, the use of the classical Greek verb (*agallein*) was too closely associated with the drunken enthusiasm of the worshippers of Dionysus, the Greek god of wine. The new word (*agallian*) is found for the first time in the Septuagint. It expresses a religious kind of joy, joy in God. It signifies spiritual exaltation or sacred rapture, being carried away in divine ecstasy.[2] This is exactly the meaning of the German word *Entzücken*, used by Luther and later writers to denote the spiritual experience of a higher joy that transports the soul.[1] So in the Septuagint the Greek verb (*agallian*) and its cognate noun (*agalliasis*) signify the joy of worship in which God is praised for his wonderful actions.

Not only so; but in the Septuagint these words belong especially to sacred song, for they are usually found in the psalms or in poetic passages of the prophets. Those who take refuge in God are exhorted to "break into shouts of *joy*" (Ps. 5:11). Psalmists are continually exulting and praising God for his goodness (see, for example, Ps. 9:1f.; 16:9; 92:4). They sing for joy on account of God's wonderful deeds and call others to "*raise a joyful song* to the Lord, a shout of triumph to the Rock of our salvation" (Ps. 95:1). Compare Isaiah 61:10—"Let me rejoice (*euphrainein*—see Chapter Three) in the Lord with all my heart, *let me exult* in my God; for he has robed me in salvation as a garment. ..."

From the Old Testament, these words for exultant joy in the worship of the God of salvation passed into the New Testament.

New Testament

The Greek verb *agallian* (= to exult) occurs eleven times in the New Testament:

Matthew	1
Luke	2
Acts	2
John	2
1 Peter	3
Revelation	1

The cognate noun *agalliasis* (= exultation, exultant joy) occurs five times:

Luke	2
Acts	1
Hebrews	1
Jude	1

It can be seen at a glance that Luke uses this Greek root more often than anyone else in the New Testament—four times in his gospel and three times in the Acts of the Apostles—seven times out of a total of sixteen instances altogether. Furthermore, the root is entirely absent from Paul's writings, Hebrews being non-Pauline.

It has been suggested that one reason for the absence of the root from Paul is his wide use of another Greek root for joy—"joyful boasting" (*kauchasthai* and its cognates—see Chapter Seven).[3] There is also an element of joy in Paul's use of the verb *katangellein* (= to proclaim) in 1 Corinthians 11:26— "For every time you eat this bread and drink the cup, *you proclaim* the death of the Lord, until he comes."

In the New Testament as in the Septuagint the Greek verb *agallian* and its cognate noun signify joy of a religious kind. It is a joy that praises God on account of his mighty acts in the past. It is also used to praise God because of promises and hopes of future glory given to men and women through Jesus Christ.

Praise of God's Goodness

The first aspect of this exuberant joy—that which magnifies God for his wonderful deeds—is clearly seen in the case of Mary, the mother of Jesus. She burst into song on account of God's goodness and mercy in promising her a son to fulfil not only her own hopes but also those of her people, Israel. "My soul magnifies the Lord, and my spirit *rejoices* in God my Saviour" (Lk.1:46f.—RSV).

Elizabeth and Zechariah demonstrate also this aspect of joy and thanksgiving to God. The angel anticipated this when foretelling the birth of John the Baptist: "And you will have joy (*chara*—see Chapter Ten) and *gladness* and many *will rejoice* at his birth" (Lk.1:14—RSV). This "thrill for joy" (NEB) was partly realised even before the birth of the promised son. When Mary came to confide in her kinswoman, Elizabeth, the latter pronounced God's blessing upon her and said: "When your greeting sounded in my ears, the baby in my womb leapt (*skirtan*—see Chapter Nine) for *joy*" (Lk.1:44).

Later on in this gospel, Luke tells us that Jesus himself parti-cipated in this aspect of exultant joy on the return of the seventy-two from their successful mission of evangelism: "Jesus *exulted* in the Holy Spirit" (Lk.10:21). This remarkable out-burst of joy on the part of Jesus was due to the fact that God had revealed divine mysteries to ordinary, common people.

God had not reserved the revelation of his fatherhood for the educated religious intelligentsia.

In his sermon on the day of Pentecost, Peter quoted Psalm 16: 8-11 to prove that even David long ago rejoiced over the wonderful acts that God was to perform through Jesus, the Messiah: "For David says of him: 'I foresaw that the presence of the Lord would be with me always ...; therefore my heart was glad (*euphrainein*—see Chapter Three) and my tongue *spoke with joy*' " (Acts 2:25f.). In the same chapter of Acts, the cognate noun (*agalliasis*) is found in a description of the Christian church after Pentecost. Exultant joy and thanksgiving were prominent characteristics of all its members as they attended the temple daily and as they met for eucharistic worship in private houses. Their very meals were festivals of exultation (Acts 2:46). This joyful living was a result of their faith in God, who had finally delivered them through his Messiah and had shown them his truth.

The third and final occurrence of the root in Acts has a similar connotation. The Philippian jailer "brought Paul and Silas into his house, set out a meal, and *rejoiced* with his whole household in his new-found faith in God" (Acts 16:34).

It is possible to see this aspect of exultant and exuberant joy in the two examples of the verb in the Fourth Gospel, though some scholars believe that here it is quite weak in meaning. Many people had felt that John the Baptist might be the long-expected Messiah and they had flocked to him—but only for a short time. Later on, Jesus reminded the Jews of the temporary popularity of his forerunner and of the fickleness of those who had been attracted to him. Like moths round a lighted candle, they had been "ready to *exult* in his light" (Jn.5:35). On another occasion, Jesus referred to the Jewish tradition according to which Abraham saw the whole history of his descendants when God established the covenant with him. "Your father Abraham *was overjoyed* to see my day" (Jn.8:56).

In the letter to the Hebrews, a quotation from Psalm 45:7 is used in order to show that Christ is superior to the angels. "Of the Son he says, 'Thy throne, O God, is for ever and ever ... therefore, O God, thy God has set thee above thy fellows, by anointing with the oil of *exultation*' " (Heb.1:8f.). If this is intended by the unknown author of Hebrews to be taken as a reference to the descent of the Holy Spirit upon Jesus[4], it would be parallel to Luke 10:21, where we are told that "Jesus *exulted* in the Holy Spirit" on the return of the seventy-two. In both cases, the Holy Spirit would then be seen as being the source of the inspiration of the exultant joy of Jesus.

Promises of Triumphant Future

In the remaining six instances of this Greek root in the New Testament, the eschatological note is struck. This is most clearly seen in the song of the redeemed in the Book of Revelation: "Exult (*chairein*—see Chapter Ten) and *shout for joy* and do him homage, for the wedding-day of the Lamb has come!" (Rev.19:7). It is also evident in 1 Peter, whose author is led to direct his readers' attention to the hope of future glory in order to strengthen them for the trials that they may shortly have to undergo. "This is *cause for great joy*, even though now you smart for a little while, if need be, under trials of many kinds" (1 Pet.1:6). When Christ's glory is revealed, "your joy *will be triumphant*" (1 Pet.4:13). In this verse, inward joy (*chara/ chairein*—see Chapter Ten) and exultant joy are combined, the latter being the outward expression of something deep within the Christian personality.

Jude also takes up the same strain of joyful triumph in the eschatological future. In his doxology at the close of his letter, he commits his readers "to the One who can keep you from falling and set you in the presence of his glory, *jubilant* and above reproach" (Jude 24).

This eschatological joy can be anticipated in faith, even in the midst of sorrows and sufferings in the present world. So the disciples were told by Jesus to accept insults and persecution "with gladness (*chara*—see Chapter Ten) and *exultation*" since they had a rich reward in heaven (Mt.5:12). This note of anticipation is also present in 1 Peter, especially in chapter one. "You have not seen him, yet you love him; and trusting in him now without seeing him, you are *transported* with a joy (*chara*) too great for words" (1 Pet.1:8).

Exultant Joy in Three Tenses

This exultant joy in the New Testament is closely linked with the joy in worship that is expressed by means of these words in the Psalter and in other parts of the Septuagint. The inward joy of the Christian (*chara*—see Chapter Ten) should find expression in joyful worship on the Lord's day.[5]

From an examination of the occurrences of the Greek verb (*agallian*) and its cognate noun (*agalliasis*) in the New Testament, we can see how this root refers to exultant joy in three tenses—past, present, and future. We Christians sing for joy because of God's wonderful deeds in the past—especially in the coming of Jesus Christ to this world of ours. We can look forward to the future with exultant joy in the present. And why can we rejoice in the present? We can do so because of our sure and certain hope of further fulfilment and realisation of our exultant joy in God in the future world.

2

OPTIMISM — THE MOOD OF FAITH
euthumein, euthumos

Classical Greek and Septuagint

In classical Greek, the most common meaning of *euthumos* was "cheerful", "in good spirits". The adverb meant "cheerfully" and the verb could be used both transitively and intransitively meaning either "to make cheerful" or "to be of good cheer".

The root occurs only once in the Septuagint—in the form of the adjective. In a letter to his brother Lysias, King Antiochus told him to inform the Jews that their temple would be restored and that they would be allowed to observe their own laws, "so that, knowing what our intentions are, they may settle down *confidently* and quietly to manage their own affairs" (2 Macc.11:26).

New Testament

There are five instances of the root in the New Testament—only once outside the Book of Acts. The verb occurs three times in all—twice in Acts (27:22, 25) and once in James: "*Is* anyone *in good heart*? He should sing praises" (Jas.5:13). The adjective and the adverb occur once each in Acts (27:36; 24:10).

An examination of these occurrences reveals that in three of
the cases in Acts the words are on the lips of the Apostle Paul.
In the fourth instance in Acts, the adjective is used to describe
the effect of Paul's speech on the people in his company (Acts
27:36).

Paul himself was always "in good spirits". Nothing could
shake his faith and trust in God, who strengthened his heart and
encouraged him even when he was in the midst of great dangers
and difficulties. Being therefore of a cheerful disposition
himself, he could give cheer and encouragement to other
people, even in the course of a storm at sea. Like Edward
Wilson in the twentieth century, Paul's faith was one "that
could read in the momentary rainbow at the height of the storm
that only he had eyes to see the hope or rather the assurance that
all was to be well".[1]

So it had been with Jesus. Though tossed about in a small
boat on the Lake of Galilee, he could sleep peacefully on a
pillow. When roused by his terror-stricken disciples, he stilled
the waves and rebuked their childish fears: "Why are you such
cowards? Have you no faith even now?" (Mk.4:40) Both in the
case of Jesus and in that of Paul, the basis of optimism in the
face of the stormy seas is to be found in their faith in God. Paul
was convinced that none on board the storm-tossed vessel
would be lost since God assured him that the lives of all would
be preserved and that he himself would stand before Caesar on
trial. Similarly, when Jesus rebuked the disciples, it was their
lack of faith that he blamed for their fearfulness (Mk.4:40). He
himself had been able to sleep on calmly until roused by them
because of his absolute trust in his heavenly Father.

3

GLADNESS or GOOD CHEER
euphrainein, euphrosunē

Classical Greek and Septuagint

This verb is very common in Greek literature from the time of Homer. In the active voice, it signified "to cheer", "to gladden", "to enjoy oneself"—particularly in connection with the joys of eating. The noun—meaning "mirth" or "merriment"—was used especially of the good cheer proper to a banquet or meal. In spite of this, both words often denoted the inner attitude or occurrence of joy. Such terms as "heart", "mind", and "spirit" are found as subjects.

In the Septuagint, both verb and noun occur very frequently. *Euphrainein* and *agallian* (see Chapter One) are often combined in the psalms. They are also used in parallel construction as synonyms. Thus *euphrainein* did not have any strictly defined meaning as opposed to *agallian*. It could designate both the individual mood of gladness over God's care and the cultic joy of the people of God assembled for worship.

Such joy among the people of God is matched by joy in the heart of God himself. In answer to the prophet's intercession for the people of Israel, God promised to create a new heaven and a new earth in which the keynote would be that of rejoicing

both by God and by the people (Isaiah 65:18f.). The eschatological element implicit here is found elsewhere in the Old
Testament. Heaven and earth are called upon by the psalmist to
share in the joy of the end-time (Ps.96:11,13; 97:1). So it is also
in 1 Chronicles, where the trees of the forest are called upon to
"shout for joy before the Lord when he comes to judge the
earth" (1 Chron.16:33).

As in classical Greek, the root also occurs in the Septuagint of
festive joy or merry-making. The wedding-feast of Tobias "was
kept seven days with great *gladness*" (Tobit 11:19). Again,
when Ezra the scribe read aloud from the book of the law on his
return to Jerusalem in the year 397 B.C., "all the people went
away to eat and to drink, to send shares to others and to
celebrate the day with great *rejoicing*, because they had
understood what had been explained to them" (Nehemiah
8:12).

Apocrypha and Pseudepigrapha

In the Apocrypha and Pseudepigrapha, the root is used both
in its cultic and in its eschatological significations. When it is
cultic joy that is at issue, the root is usually connected with a
festival. As a result, in its cultic signification *euphrosunē* is also
"festive joy". Thus, in 1 Esdras, the children of Israel who
came out of captivity "kept the Feast of Unleavened Bread for
seven days, *rejoicing* before the Lord" (1 Esdras 7:14). Several
examples of this cultic joy are found in the Books of the
Maccabees. When Judas Maccabaeus destroyed the abomina-
tion of desolation that had been set up in the temple court at
Jerusalem in 168 B.C. and rededicated the altar to Yahweh
exactly three years after its destruction by Antiochus Epiphanes,
the people celebrated the event with great rejoicing (1 Macc.
4:59). The joy of worship is also apparent in 3 Maccabees in the
account of a service of praise and thanksgiving to God for his
deliverance of the people (3 Macc.7:16).

The eschatological note is struck in the course of Tobit's
prayer of rejoicing: "How happy shall they all be who grieve for
you in your afflictions; they shall rejoice over you and for ever
be witness of your *joy*" (Tobit 13:14). It is also found
frequently in the Testaments of the Twelve Patriarchs.

Philo makes much of the root in its festive sense and

distinguishes between legitimate and illegitimate merrymaking. Only the wise and prudent man knows truly how to celebrate with joy, and good cheer follows as a result of seeking God, who lets joy stream out of heaven. Indeed, it is God alone who has genuine joy. In his relationships with men, God's *euphrosunē* is the greatest good, for he is glad in those who, through their virtues, are worthy of his gifts.

New Testament

The root occurs only sixteen times in the New Testament. Of these, ten are in Luke-Acts, three in the Pauline letters and three in the Book of Revelation. The noun appears twice in Acts; the rest of the appearances of the root in the New Testament are of the verb.

	Noun	*Verb*
Luke	—	6
Acts	2	2
Paul	—	3
Revelation	—	3

In Luke's Gospel, as in modern Greek[1], the verb *euphrainein* always occurs with the baser significance of festive merrymaking. First of all, in the parable of the rich fool there occurs what has been called "an epicurean asyndeton"[2], in which the rich man addresses himself: "Man, you have plenty of good things laid by, enough for many years: take life easy, eat, drink and *enjoy yourself*" (Lk.12:19). In the course of the parable of the prodigal son, the verb is used four times with this meaning. When the foolish young man returned home with a speech of repentance upon his lips, the father welcomed him with open arms and gave orders to the servants to bring the best clothes they could and to prepare a banquet in honour of his penitent son: "Let us have a feast to *celebrate the day*" (Lk.15:23). The robe, the ring, the shoes, the fatted calf were all part of the welcome home and signs of the prodigal's forgiveness and reconciliation with his father. The climax came in the festive joy in the father's house when "the festivities began" (Lk.15:24). The music and the dancing of the celebrations came to the elder son's ears as he approached the house after his day's work in the field, and he refused to share in the general rejoicing over the return of the prodigal. He complained bitterly that he had never been given so much as a kid "for a feast" (Lk.15:29) with his friends. In the face of the elder son's rebukes, the father proclaimed his love for both his sons and upheld the propriety of his actions: "How could we help *celebrating* this happy day?" (Lk.15:32). The last example of the verb in Luke's Gospel comes in the story of the rich man and Lazarus. We are told that the rich man "*feasted* in great magnificence every day" (Lk.16:19).

In the Acts of the Apostles, there are two examples of the use of the verb. In the course of his sermon on the Day of Pentecost, Peter quoted part of Psalm 16 as referring to the resurrection of Christ: "Therefore my heart *was glad* and my tongue rejoiced (*agallian*) ..." (Acts 2:26). Here, *euphrainein* refers to a joyous state of mind while *agallian* is used of the outward and active expression of that joy. This is in spite of the fact that elsewhere in the New Testament, and also in the Septuagint, the root could be used of festive enjoyment as an outward expression.

The second example of the verb in Acts occurs, like the first, in a reference to the Old Testament. In his defence, Stephen talks of the refusal of the Israelites to obey Moses: "They made the bull-calf, and offered sacrifice to the idol, and *held a feast* in honour of the thing their hands had made" (Acts 7:41). In his comment on this verse, Bengel remarks that God rejoices in the works of his own hands, while we should rejoice in the works of God's hands, whereas (as here) idolators are men who rejoice in the works of their own hands.[3]

The Book of Acts also contains the only two instances of the noun *euphrosunē* in the New Testament. The first appears in the quotation from Psalm 16 already mentioned. In the course of his sermon, Peter goes on to quote: "Thou hast shown me the ways of life, thou wilt fill me with *gladness* by thy presence" (Acts 2:28). A certain eschatological element is implicit here since "the psalmist's thoughts carried him beyond mere temporal deliverance, beyond the changes and chances of this mortal life, to the assurance of a union with God, which death could not dissolve; while as Christians we read with St Peter a deeper and a fuller meaning still in the words, as we recall the

Life, Death, Resurrection, and Ascension" of Jesus Christ.[4]

The association of the root with eating comes out in Acts 14:17 in the course of Paul's instructions to the people of Lystra concerning God the Creator who "has not left you without some clue to his nature, in the kindness he shows: he sends you rain from heaven and crops in their seasons, and gives you food and *good cheer* in plenty." *Euphrosunē* can thus be regarded gratefully as the gift of God himself, who satisfies all the needs of human beings.

Paul uses the verb twice within quotations from the Old Testament to show how the Gentiles have as good grounds for glorifying God as have the Jews. Since Christ was God's gift to all men, to the Jew first but also to the Gentiles, they should welcome one another as brothers. "As Scripture says: '... Gentiles, *make merry* together with his own people' " (Rom.15:10). In Galatians, the Apostle quotes Isaiah 54:1 as witness to the greater favour of the people of promise over the people of law: "For Scripture says, '*Rejoice*, O barren woman who never bore child ...' " (Gal.4:27). In this description of "the deserted wife" who "shall have more children than she who lives with the husband", there is an image "peculiarly appropriate for describing the long delayed but fertile growth of the Christian Church".[5]

In 2 Corinthians, Paul uses the verb in the sense of the joy that can come from human relationships that are mutually pleasant. "If I cause pain to you, who is left to *cheer me up*, except you, whom I have offended?" (2 Cor.2:2). The Apostle had intended visiting the Christians at Corinth but had changed his plans since, if he had visited them, they would have saddened him. He would then have been grieved by those who were the source of his purest joy.

The root is found once again in the sense of merrymaking in the Book of Revelation, where John the Seer has a vision of the death of the two faithful witnesses and of the consequent rejoicing of the earth-dwellers who had been troubled by their prophecies: "All men on earth gloat over them, *make merry*, and exchange presents; for these two prophets were a torment to the whole earth" (Rev.11:10). The remaining two instances of the root in Revelation are in line with the Old Testament summons to exultant joy in face of the eschatological judgments of God. The heavens and all that they contain are called upon to take part in the general rejoicing over the victory of Christ (Rev.12:12) and the people of God are encouraged to share in the joy of the heavens over the defeat of the great city (Rev.18:20).

Summary

By way of summary we can say, firstly, that the root is used in the New Testament as in classical Greek of an inner state of mind in contrast to the outward expression of joy contained in *agallian* and its cognates (see Chapter One). The objects of this *good cheer* can be either right or wrong. Thus, men should not rejoice in the works of their hands (as did the Israelites quoted by Stephen in Acts 7:41) or in any created things, but should take their delight in God alone, being full of gladness in his presence (Acts 2:28), both here and hereafter.

Secondly, the root is used along with such things as eating and drinking to signify the material things that are considered as of primary importance by the earthly man who forgets God. So the rich man "feasted in great magnificence every day" (Lk.16:19) and the rich fool imagined that he could make sure of his happiness in life by adding to his possessions (Lk.12:19). He forgot that any food and cheer he might have were gifts of God (Acts 14:17).

Through this conception of joy in eating, the root moves out into the external significance of festive joy that the noun possessed in particular in earlier times. This thought of merrymaking at a feast is found in the root in papyri of the second and third centuries A.D.[6], and in modern Greek.

Finally, the eschatological element apparent in the root in the Septuagint, especially in the Psalter, is introduced into the New Testament scene in the Book of Revelation, where the whole of God's creation is summoned to share in the *good cheer* of the end-time on account of the victory of Christ and the eschatological judgments of God himself.

4

PLEASURE
hēdonē, hēdus, hēdeōs

Classical Greek

Hēdonē and the adjective *hēdus* are both probably derived from the same Sanskrit root *suad*, which gives *suavis* in Latin, *swete* in Anglo-Saxon and "sweet" in English.

Hēdonē itself is a word that occurs very frequently in classical Greek in the sense of "delight", "enjoyment", or "pleasure". It is properly used of sensuous pleasure and can denote the lusts of the flesh, as in Xenophon, Plato and Aristotle. It is also found, however, in a more neutral sense of the pleasure obtained from hearing something pleasant. Hence it came to be used in the early Ionic philosophers of the sensible quality of a body, e.g., its taste, smell, or flavour. In the Epicurean system of philosophy, pleasure was the chief end of man, though as understood by Epicurus it was mainly a negative term and implied the absence of pain and suffering.

The adverb *hēdeōs* is also a common word in classical Greek and in hellenistic Greek. There are several instances of it in the Oxyrhynchus papyri. There is also an interesting example of its use in a letter written by the Emperor Claudius to thank a gymnastic club for the gift of a golden crown sent to him to commemorate his victory over the Britons: "I received *with pleasure* the golden crown which you sent to me in connection with my victory over the Britons."[1] The superlative form occurs fairly frequently in classical Greek.

Septuagint

There are several examples of the use of the root in the Septuagint. As in the early Ionic philosophers, the noun occurs with the meaning of "taste". When the Israelites had boiled the manna and made cakes of it, "it *tasted* like butter-cakes" (Num.11:8). Manna is referred to again in the Wisdom of Solomon—"bread ready to eat, rich in delight of every kind and suited to their *taste*" (Wisdom 16:20). There is another occurrence of the noun in the Wisdom of Solomon, where we hear of "*pleasure* that is joined with sleep" (Wisdom 7:2).

The adverb, too, appears in the Septuagint; for example, in Proverbs 3:24 — "When you lie down, your sleep will be *pleasant*."

New Testament

In the New Testament, the root occurs ten times:

	Noun	Verb
Mark	—	2
Luke	1	—
Paul	—	3
Titus	1	—
James	2	—
2 Peter	1	—

The noun *hēdonē* appears five times, the first being in the course of Jesus' exposition of the parable of the seed and the soils. The seed that fell among the thistles are "those who hear, but their further growth is choked by cares and wealth and the *pleasures* of life, and they bring nothing to maturity" (Lk.8:14). The word bears a similar meaning in Titus 3:3—"We were slaves to passions and *pleasures* of every kind." The term translated here by "passions" (*epithumiai*) means literally "desires". In the letter of James, the plural of *hēdonē* itself is twice used with this meaning: "What causes conflicts and quarrels among you? Do they not spring from the aggressiveness of your bodily *desires?* ... Your requests are not granted because you pray from wrong motives, to spend what you get on your *pleasures*" (Jas.4:1,3). Finally, in 2 Peter the noun occurs in the singular: "To carouse in broad daylight is their idea of *pleasure*" (2 Pet.2:13).

Thus, while in classical Greek the word could have both a good and a bad significance and while in the Septuagint it is usually morally neutral, in the New Testament the noun has the baser, sensual meaning of wordly passions and pleasure.

The adverb *hēdēos* is found twice in Mark's Gospel. Herod "*liked* to listen to John, although the listening left him greatly perplexed" (Mk.6:20). Whereas here it is the words of John the Baptist that give joy to the person hearing them, in the second instance it is what a greater than John has to say that produces this result. As Jesus disputed with the religious leaders who came to him with their trick questions, "there was a great crowd and they listened *eagerly*" (Mk.12:37). In the first example, the joy of Herod is mixed with a certain perplexity and fear, since John the Baptist had denounced him and Herodias in no uncertain terms. Nevertheless, Herod had a delight in hearing the Baptist, for "there is a flashy joy, which a hypocrite may have in hearing the word; Ezekiel was to his hearers as a 'lovely song' (Ezek.33:32); and the 'stony ground received the word with joy'[2] (Lk.8:13)."[3] On the other hand, the common people of Palestine were genuinely pleased with the teaching of Jesus. He spoke to them about God and the things of the kingdom as one who had authority. In debates with the recognized religious leaders of the day, he always came off best. Those who dared to argue with him were invariably discomfited.

A third example of the adverb occurs in 2 Corinthians: "How *gladly* you bear with fools, being yourselves so wise!" (2 Cor.11:19) Thus Paul appeals to the Corinthians, in their wisdom, to bear with him patiently in his folly in boasting (2 Cor.11:16-18—*kauchasthai*—see Chapter Seven) of the difficulties and dangers he has had to endure as an apostle of Jesus Christ.

This letter also contains the only two examples of the use of the superlative adverb in the New Testament. They occur within a few verses of each other and in a similar connection to that in which the adverb occurs in the last text quoted, i.e., in connection with Paul's boasting concerning his weaknesses: "I shall therefore *prefer* to find my joy and pride in the very things that are my weakness; and then the power of Christ will come and rest upon me. ... I will *gladly* spend what I have for you—yes, and spend myself to the limit" (2 Cor.12:9,15).

This superlative adverb is found in some inferior manuscripts in an addition to the text of Acts 13:8. In the course of their first missionary journey, Paul and Barnabas visited the island of Cyprus. At Paphos, they were summoned by Sergius Paulus, the Roman proconsul, who "wanted to hear the word of God" (Acts 13:7). Elymas the sorcerer, however, opposed the apostles, "trying to turn the governor away from the faith, since he had heard them *very gladly*." As in the case of Herod and the common people in the Mark's Gospel, the cause of the joy is the hearing of the word of God. Paul, however, appears to have had more positive results than did John the Baptist or even Jesus with the vast majority of the Jewish people who heard them gladly; for we are told that "the governor ... became a believer, deeply impressed by what he learned about the Lord" (Acts 13:12). There is little merit in simply hearing the gospel message gladly. Unless that joy in hearing leads on to joy in believing in Christ and in service for him, one might as well not have heard the word of God gladly.

Summary

While the noun, in all five of its occurrences in the New Testament, has the baser significance that is contained in the root, the adverb does not always necessarily have that connotation. The gladness of hearing the message of the gospel is all very well so far as it goes, but before it can have any real worth it must lead on to belief in Jesus Christ as the Son of God. There can be a glad hearing that is too superficial and too shallow. It is crushed out of existence by the cares and pleasures of this world; for

> ... pleasures are like poppies spread—
> You seize the flower, its bloom is shed;
> Or like the snow falls in the river—
> A moment white—then melts for ever.[4]

The Apostle Paul, on the other hand, not only heard the word of God in Jesus Christ but acted upon it. As a result, he came to the point where he could actually boast of his own weakness— and boast in gladness. He could gladly spend and be spent in service for Christ for the salvation of men and women.

5

COURAGE
tharsein, tharrein, tharsos

Classical Greek

Tharsein, of which the later New Attic form is *tharrein*, appears frequently in Greek literature from the time of Homer. It means "to be of good courage", "to have confidence in" someone or something, or "to have confidence against", i.e., "to disdain", "to have no fear of". The imperative occurs in the sense of "cheer up!" "take courage!" The cognate noun *tharsos* is found in Homer and in Attic Greek with the meaning of "courage".

The root occurs very often in Plato, especially in the *Phaedo*. This dialogue takes place between Socrates and his friends just prior to his death by drinking hemlock. Its subject is the question of the immortality of the soul, namely, whether it is possible "to *feel confident* that, when we die, our soul still continues in existence somewhere" (88b). In the course of the argument, Socrates tries to unfold to his friends "the reason why a man who has in reality spent his life in the pursuits of philosophy, appears to me to *be fearless* and undaunted when about to die, and to cherish a favourable hope that when he dies, he shall in that other state obtain the greatest possible

38

blessings" (63e). Finally, he concludes that "for the sake of these things, that man should entertain a *confident* hope in regard to his own soul, who, during life, has neglected other pleasures ... but has earnestly prosecuted the pleasures of learning ..." (114d).

Septuagint

The verb is found twenty-eight times in the Septuagint, usually in the form *tharsein*. Only three times do we find the later form *tharrein*—in Daniel and in 4 Maccabees. Except in two passages in the Book of Proverbs (1:21 and 31:11), the verb always occurs in the Old Testament in the imperative form, either singular or plural.

In Proverbs 31:11, the root has the meaning of "trust" and is followed by a preposition. Speaking of the good wife, the writer says, "The heart of her husband *trusts* in her, and he will have no lack of gain." Elsewhere in the Old Testament, as also in the rest of the Septuagint, the root signifies "to be of good cheer", "not to be afraid", usually in the imperative form.

Almost without exception, the reason for the command "be of good cheer" or "fear not" is to be found in God and in his mighty acts or promises. Thus, on two separate occasions, Moses exhorts the children of Israel with the word *tharseite* in the Septuagint. When they were being pursued by Pharaoh and his army before they crossed the Red Sea, Moses said: *"Have no fear*; stand firm and see the deliverance that the Lord will bring you this day"* (Ex.14:13). Again, when they stood terror-stricken before Mount Sinai, listening to the thunder and watching the lightning, Moses said: *"Do not be afraid.* God has come only to test you ..." (Ex.20:20). The prophet Joel addresses his exhortation, *"Be not afraid"*, to the world of nature—earth and cattle in the field—"for the Lord himself has done a proud deed ... the pastures shall be green ..." (Joel 2:21f.). The post-exilic prophet Zechariah encourages the people to rebuild the temple in Jerusalem by telling them of God's purpose to bless them. *"Courage! ... Do not be afraid"* (Zech.8:13,15). Haggai also encourages the people, but he introduces an additional idea to comfort and to strengthen them: "My spirit is present among you. *Have no fear"* (Hag.2:5).

An eschatological element appears once in connection with the root in the Old Testament: "On that day this shall be the message to Jerusalem: *Fear not*, O Zion; let not your hands fall slack" (Zeph.3:16).

The Apocrypha contains sixteen examples of the imperative of the verb, half of them occurring in the two books of Tobit and Judith. The Wisdom of Ben Sirach contains an interesting warning against idle gossiping: "Have you heard a rumour? Let it die with you. *Never fear*, it will not make you burst" (Sir.19:10).

A papyrus fragment from the second century, B.C., gives us another instance of the imperative singular: "Eye of my soul, *take courage.*"[1]

New Testament

In the New Testament, the verb appears in the form *tharsein* seven times in the Gospels and Acts, always in the imperative mood. It appears in the later form *tharrein* five times in 2 Corinthians and once in the Letter to the Hebrews. The cognate noun *tharsos* is found only once—in the Acts of the Apostles.

	Tharsein	*Tharrein*	*Tharsos*
Matthew	3	—	—
Mark	2	—	—
John	1	—	—
Acts	1	—	1
Paul	—	5	—
Hebrews	—	1	—

Gospels and Acts

On six of the seven occasions when the imperative—either singular or plural—occurs in the Gospels and Acts, it is found on the lips of Jesus, and on the seventh occasion it is used by the crowd as a result of what Jesus has said.

The first example is in Matthew's Gospel when a paralytic was brought to Jesus by some friends. "Seeing their faith Jesus said to the man, '*Take heart*, my son; your sins are forgiven' " (Mt.9:2). Mark and Luke also record the incident, including some details omitted by Matthew; but neither of these two evangelists puts this imperative *tharsei* on the lips of Jesus. It is

Matthew alone who gives us this word on this occasion.

Later on in the same chapter, the word is found once again on the lips of Jesus, this time when speaking to the woman with the haemorrhage who touched the edge of his cloak. Turning round to her, Jesus said: *"Take heart*, my daughter; your faith has cured you" (Mt.9:22). Parallel accounts of this incident are given in Mark and in Luke, but in neither of them is the verb *tharsein* used (Mk.5:34; Lk.8:48).

Following upon the account of the feeding of the five thousand, there comes in both Matthew and Mark the story of how Jesus came to the disciples walking over the lake. The superstitious young men were terrified, thinking that it was a ghost making up on them to bring about their destruction. Jesus immediately calmed their fears and comforted their hearts with his shout of assurance: *"Take heart!* It is I; do not be afraid" (Mt.14:27 = Mk.6:50). Thus it was over the very waves and storms that were distressing them that Jesus came to the disciples and so asserted the divine supremacy even there. The encounter with Jesus Christ was something that could free them from fears concerning the difficulties and dangers which they had to face in the course of their everyday life.

This fact comes out again in the story of blind Bartimaeus who was sitting by the roadside as Jesus left Jericho one day with his disciples. In response to an appeal, Jesus summoned him to his side. The people recognized that even the interest of Jesus in anyone was sufficient grounds for his being of good cheer. They said to the blind man: *"Take heart*, stand up; he is calling you" (Mk.10:49). The result of this meeting with Jesus was that Bartimaeus was freed from his bodily disease and received his sight. His faith in Christ had made him well again. So it had been also in the case of the woman with the haemorrhage (Mt.9:22), though in the story of the paralytic (Mt.9:2), it was the faith of his four friends that had helped towards the cure.

The imperative plural occurs once in the Fourth Gospel within the context of the farewell discourses. Though threatened by persecution and martyrdom and though living in the anxiety of the time before the crucifixion, the disciples are summoned by Jesus to have peace and to be of good cheer. "I have told you all this so that in me you may find peace. In the

world you will have trouble. But *courage*! The victory is mine; I
have conquered the world" (Jn.16:33). The possession of peace
and joy in the face of tribulation and peril is founded upon, and
proved by, the example of Jesus himself. The disciples remain in
the hands of the Victor over the cosmos and therefore need have
no fear of anything that comes out of the cosmos.[2]

Thus, while Socrates affirmed that the philosopher could
maintain confidence in face of the last threat to existence on
account of what he carried within himself, the immortality of
the soul, Christianity maintains confidence through Christ's
victory in overcoming the world. This victory was gained by
Christ's death on the cross and by his resurrection.

Although the root *tharsein* does not occur again in the Fourth
Gospel, the same counsel is given in different words, especially
in chapter fourteen: "Set your troubled hearts at rest. Trust in
God always; trust also in me" (Jn.14:1).[3]

The imperative singular appears once in the Acts of the
Apostles. After Paul's arrest and imprisonment in Jerusalem,
"the Lord appeared to him and said, '*Keep up your courage*;
you have affirmed the truth about me in Jerusalem, and you
must do the same in Rome' " (Acts 23:11). The word that had
already brought cheer during the earthly life of Jesus to the sick
and diseased, to the storm-tossed disciples on the Lake of
Galilee, and to those same disciples in an hour of even greater
need, now brought comfort to the heart of the imprisoned
apostle as it issued from the lips of his risen Lord and Master.

The root occurs once again in the Acts of the Apostles in the
form of the noun *tharsos*. Paul's arrival at Rome is being
described. Luke tells us that when the Roman Christians heard
that the apostle was approaching they "came out to meet us as
far as Appii Forum and Tres Tabernae, and when Paul saw
them, he gave thanks to God and took *courage*" (Acts 28:15).
The promise made by the risen Christ to him in prison at
Jerusalem was now in process of being fulfilled. His joy at
seeing and meeting some of the members of the Church at Rome
made him forget the trials he had been through in the course of
the journey from Jerusalem.

Paul and Hebrews

Tharrein, the later form of the verb, appears six times in the

New Testament and five of these are in Paul—in 2 Corinthians.

First of all, Paul recognizes the possibility of being of good courage in the present life even though Christ is no longer with us in the same way as he was with the disciples during his life on earth. "We never cease *to be confident.* We know that so long as we are at home in the body we are exiles from the Lord; faith is our guide, we do not see him. *We are confident,* I repeat, and would rather leave our home in the body and go to live with the Lord" (2 Cor.5:6-8). In contrast to the philosophical hopes of Socrates, based on his reflections as to the possibility of the immortality of the soul, Paul is radiantly confident in the face of death and is even desirous of it; for he is absolutely certain that for a man who is "in Christ" now, death simply means going home to be "with Christ" in the hereafter. Thus the basis of Paul's cheerfulness throughout life is to be found in his great conviction that there is "nothing in all creation that can separate us from the love of God in Christ Jesus our Lord" (Rom.8:39).

Paul also uses this root to express his hopeful confidence in the Christians at Corinth. "How happy I am (*chairein*—see Chapter Ten) now to have complete *confidence* in you!" (2 Cor.7:16) Later on, the verb occurs twice to express Paul's "confidence against" or "disdain of" his critics at Corinth—a sense that is found only here in the New Testament, though it is quite common in classical Greek, as we have already seen. "I, Paul, appeal to you ... I, so feeble (you say) when I am face to face with you, so *brave* when I am away. Spare me, I beg you, the necessity of such *bravery* when I come ..." (2 Cor.10:1,2).

Finally, the verb appears once in the participial form in the letter to the Hebrews. After warning his readers against avarice and after advising them to be content with what they have on the ground that they have the divine promise, the author introduces a quotation from Psalm 118:6 by writing: "So we can *take courage* and say, 'The Lord is my helper, I will not fear; what can man do to me?' " (Heb.13:6).

Conclusion

In the introduction to George Seaver's biography of Edward Wilson[4], we are told that this is "the story of a man who, however appalling the conditions, and whatever the dangers, in the face of starvation and more than once of inevitable death, just went on doing his job..." It is a story which "will give you courage".

Even more so, the gospel is a story that can give courage. By means of this root, we are shown how Jesus brought good cheer to people. He gave salvation in three tenses by assuring them of forgiveness for their past sins (Mt.9:2), by giving them strength for living in his presence always (Mt.9:22; 14:27 = Mk.6:50), and by offering them hope for the future (Jn.16:33; 2 Cor.5:6).

6

HILARITY
hilaros, hilarotēs

Classical Greek

Hilaros occurs in classical Greek with the meanings of "cheerful", "merry", "joyous". It is found in Latin as *hilaris*. In Aristophanes (*Frogs* 455), daylight is described as being *hilaros*, but elsewhere other things are spoken of as being "cheerful" or "joyous"; for example, songs, hope, or a message. The word is used, however, especially of human beings. Its opposite is *skuthrōpos* (= "of a gloomy countenance"). The cognate noun, *hilarotēs* (= "cheerfulness", "gaiety"), passes into Latin as *hilaritas* and into English as "hilarity".

On one or two occasions, we find this quality being ascribed to gods. So Demetrius, as the manifestation of the deity, is himself "cheerful".[1] One of the Oxyrhynchus papyri of the second century A.D. ascribes "a cheerful face" to the goddess Isis.[2]

Septuagint

The adjective occurs seven times in the Septuagint and the noun once. On four of these occasions, *hilaros* is found along

45

with the noun *prosōpon* (= face). For example, Esther's face
was "cheerful" as she went to interview the king (Esther 5:1—
LXX only) and man comes into God's presence with "cheerful"
face (Job 33:26—LXX only). The Book of Proverbs tells us that
"God praises a *cheerful* man and a giver", which amounts to,
"God praises a *cheerful* giver" (Prov.22:8—LXX only). The
neuter adjective is once used as a noun meaning "favour": "A
king's rage is like a lion's roar, his *favour* like dew on the grass"
(Prov.19:12). The cognate noun also bears this significance on
its solitary occurrence: "Find a wife, and you find a good thing;
so you will earn the *favour* of the Lord" (Prov.18:22).

Once in the Psalms and more often in the Wisdom of Ben
Sirach, we find the verb *hilarunein* or *hilaroun* in the sense of
"to make cheerful". Thus, we read that God gives "wine to
gladden men's hearts" (Ps.104:15), that "a woman's beauty
makes a man *happy*" (Sir.36:22), and that "dew *brings welcome relief* after heat" (Sir.43:22). Especially interesting in view
of New Testament usage is a longer passage in which "a
cheerful face" is mentioned in connection with an exhortation
to liberality in one's giving to God. "Be generous in your
worship of the Lord and present the firstfruits of your labour in
full measure. Give all your gifts *cheerfully* and be glad
(*euphrosunē*—See Chapter Three) to dedicate your tithe. ... For
the Lord always repays; you will be repaid seven times over"
(Sir.35:8-11). This connection between cheerfulness and
liberality is also insisted upon by the rabbis: "He who gives
alms, let him do so with a *cheerful* heart."[3]

New Testament

The root occurs only twice in the New Testament—the
adjective once and the noun once.

Paul gives a very free rendering of Proverbs 22:8 (LXX). He
substitutes *agapan* (= to love) for the verb *eulogein* (= to
praise) and also makes the adjective *hilaros* qualify directly the
noun *dotēs* (= giver), thus: "God loves a *cheerful* giver" (2
Cor.9:7). In making these changes, Paul does not materially
alter the sense of the verse. He has been urging the Christians at
Corinth to be generous in their support of the collection for the
church at Jerusalem. He exhorts each individual to make up his
own mind, keeping in view the fact that "sparse sowing" results

in "sparse reaping" (2 Cor.9:6). Their contribution must be given freely. "There should be no reluctance, no sense of compulsion; God loves a *cheerful* giver" (2 Cor.9:7). Thereafter, the apostle proceeds to indicate the reasons for, or the inspiration of, this cheerful giving, namely, that God himself has been generous in providing them with every blessing in abundance and, above all, in sending to them "his gift beyond words" in Jesus Christ (2 Cor.9:15).

In the letter to the Romans, Paul links cheerfulness with Christian service. In the previous verses, he has been comparing the members of the Church with various parts of the body. He has emphasized the fact that different people have different gifts from God. Each person should see to it that he uses his gifts to the best of his ability. "If you give to charity, give with all your heart; if you are a leader, exert yourself to lead; if you are helping others in distress, do it *cheerfully*" (Rom.12:8). The last two clauses are translated by James Moffatt as, "the sick visitor must be *cheerful*"; and James Denney comments: "A person of a grudging or despondent mood has not the endowment for showing mercy. He who is to visit the poor, the sick, the sorrowful, will be marked out by God for his special ministry by this endowment of brightness and good cheer."[4]

The phrase, "helping others in distress" (NEB), is translated as "he who does acts of mercy" in some versions (for example, AV and RSV). It has a wider significance than "sick-visiting" or any kind of visiting. It includes such things as the help rendered by the Good Samaritan to the man who fell among thieves. The parable of the last judgment (Mt.25:31-46) also enumerates "acts of mercy"—giving food to the hungry, drink to the thirsty, hospitality to strangers, as well as visiting the sick and those in prison. These, and all other deeds of compassion, are to be done *cheerfully*.

The necessity of linking liberality and service with cheerfulness was recognized by Gentiles and by Jews as well as by Christians. The originality of the Christian view lay in the new motivation. It is the reception of the gift of God in Jesus Christ that makes the Christian joyful. It is this supreme gift that inspires him to be cheerful in his outpouring of the love of God in his heart (cf. Rom.5:5) in acts of mercy and of love towards God and towards his neighbour. Thus Paul, at the very beginning of the ethical section of his letter to the Romans, appeals to his readers "by God's mercy to offer your very selves to him: a living sacrifice, dedicated and fit for his acceptance, the worship offered by mind and heart" (Rom.12:1). With this we can compare the words of Jesus when sending out the twelve on their mission of evangelism to "the lost sheep of the house of Israel": "Heal the sick, raise the dead, cleanse the lepers, cast out devils. You received without cost; give without charge" (Mt.10:8).

Summary

To sum up; *hilaros* and its cognates are found in classical Greek to denote "cheerfulness"—perhaps even "hilarity". In the Septuagint and in Judaism, they came to be associated with the generous giving of benefits. In the New Testament, they appear solely in connection with "cheerfulness" or "hilarity" in outpouring love—the characteristic of a Christian heart made cheerful by the example of God himself in "hilarious" giving. As G.K. Chesterton has put it somewhere: "No man can be joyful except the serious man. The thing called high spirits is only possible to the spiritual. Ultimately a man cannot rejoice in anything except the nature of things: a man can enjoy nothing except religion."

7

BOASTING
kauchasthai (and its compounds) *kauchēma, kauchēsis*

Classical Greek

Kauchasthai is first attested in the works of Sappho, Pindar and Herodotus. It is not found in the best Attic prose. From its use by comic writers, it would appear to have been a colloquial Attic term.

Akin to it in meaning are *auchein* (used by Homer and the writers of tragedy) and *euchesthai* in certain cases. This latter word means primarily "to pray", and then "to vow" or "to promise" to do something; hence "to boast" or "to vaunt". When, however, *euchesthai* is used in the sense of boasting it is found "mostly not of empty boasting, but of something of which one has a right to boast".[1]

Kauchēma (= the thing boasted of) and *kauchēsis* (= the act of boasting) are both very rare in classical Greek.

Kauchasthai (= to boast) usually has the derogatory meaning of "to brag"; as, for example, in Herodotus 7:39—"You will never *boast* that you outdid your king in the matter of benefits." There is also a maxim in Pindar: "To speak evil of the gods is a skill that is hateful, and untimely *boasting* (an articular infinitive) is in unison with madness" (*Olympic Odes*

9:58). A warning appears among the counsels of the sage Sosiades: "Let me not *boast* of my strength."[2]

Septuagint

In the Septuagint, *kauchasthai* and its cognates appear over sixty times. The element of boasting contained in the root is often criticized. The psalmist, for example, speaks derogatorily of those who "trust in their riches and *boast* of their great wealth" (Ps.49:6). He asks impatiently: "How long shall the wicked *exult*?" (Ps.94:3)

Scattered throughout the Old Testament, there are proverbial warnings against bragging. "Let not him that girds on his armour *boast himself* as he that puts it off" (1 Kings 20:11—RSV). "Like clouds and wind that bring no rain is the man who boasts of gifts he never gives" (Prov.25:14). "Do not *flatter* yourself about tomorrow, for you never know what a day will bring forth" (Prov.27:1). On the other hand, the Old Testament also knows something of a boasting or a pride that is justifiable. "Grey hair is a crown of *glory*, and it is won by a virtuous life" (Prov.16:31). "Grandchildren are the crown of old age, and sons are *proud* of their fathers" (Prov.17:6). Similarly, "a beautiful crown" is one that can be boasted about. It is, literally, "a crown of *boasting*" (Ezek.16:12;23:42).

Kauchasthai can also have a more religious connotation in the Septuagint. In contrast to the self-glory that is characteristic of the foolish and the ungodly, the pious Israelite can boast of God's beneficent acts (see, for example, 1 Chron.16:35). "Let all who take refuge in thee rejoice (*euphrainesthai*—see Chapter Three), let them for ever break into shouts of joy (*agallian*—see Chapter One); shelter those who love thy name, that they may *exult* in thee" (Ps.5:11). As we see from this example, *kauchasthai* can be found along with other words for "joy" in the Septuagint (cf. Ps.32:11). Thus there is a strong element of joy in this root for "boasting".

This "joyful boasting" is also recognized as being an essential element in the character of God himself. "Thine, O Lord, is the greatness, the power, the *glory* (*kauchēma*), the splendour, and the majesty ..." (1 Chron.29:11). "Majesty and splendour attend him, might and *joy* (*kauchēma*) are in his dwelling" (1 Chron.16:27).

Both the right and the wrong kinds of boasting are found contrasted in two famous verses from Jeremiah: "Let not the wise man *boast* of his wisdom, nor the valiant man of his valour; let not the rich man *boast* of his riches; but if any man would *boast*, let him *boast* of this, that he understands and knows me. For I am the Lord ... (Jeremiah 9:23f.).

Apocrypha and Pseudepigrapha

These same lines of interpretation of the root are retained in the Apocrypha, as well as in the other parts of the Septuagint, and in the Pseudepigrapha. Here we find not only "joyous exultation in God" but also the less exalted connotation of the root. For example, God is asked not to punish Israel by means of lawless men in case they should *boast* of their victory over God's people (3 Macc.2:17). The Testaments of the Twelve Patriarchs contain several warnings against self-glory. It is an evil spirit—the spirit of pride—that causes men to *boast* and be arrogant (Reuben 3:5) and Judah counsels his sons not to *glory* in the deeds and the strength of youth since self-glory leads into sin (Judah 13:2f.).

"Bragging", however, is balanced by true "boasting" that is grounded in God and in his acts. "The rich, the famous, and the poor—their only *boast* is the fear of the Lord" (Sir.10:22). In the Book of Judith, the heroine is described as "the glory of Jerusalem, the heroine of Israel, the *proud boast* of our people" (Jud.15:9); but in her song of thanksgiving in the following chapter she herself rejoices in God who has wrought such mighty acts of deliverance through her.

Ben Sirach knows another legitimate ground for glorying, namely, the Law. The wise man is he who "will disclose what he has learnt from his own education, and will *take pride* in the law of the Lord's covenant" (Sir.39:8). Wisdom herself *"speaks with pride* among her people" (Sir.24:1), since, for Ben Sirach, Wisdom is embodied in the Law of God.

The thoughts of this writer are echoed in the rabbinical works. The Torah is regarded as the jewel and crown of Israel. In addition, there appears in the works of the rabbis the idea that pious men should rejoice in their sufferings and thank God for them since they bring them the consciousness of God's care and also expiation for sins.[3]

New Testament

The verb *kauchasthai* and its cognates occur sixty-four times in the New Testament. Of these occurrences, no less than ninety per cent are found within the writings of Paul.

	kauchasthai	*kata-*	*en-*	*kauchēma*	*kauchēsis*
Paul	35	2	1	10	10
Hebrews	—	—	—	1	—
James	2	2	—	—	1

The simple verb *kauchasthai* occurs thirty-seven times, but in addition it is found compounded with prepositions—*kata-kauchasthai* (4 times) and *enkauchasthai* (once). There are only six examples of the use of the root outside the Pauline letters. The root is therefore used predominantly by Paul in the New Testament.[4]

It is also interesting to notice the spread of the cognates within Paul's writings:

	kauchasthai	*kata-*	*en-*	*kauchēma*	*kauchēsis*	Totals
Romans	5	2	—	1	2	10
1 Cor.	6	—	—	3	1	10
2 Cor.	20	—	—	3	6	29
Gal.	2	—	—	1	—	3
Ephes.	1	—	—	—	—	1
Phil.	1	—	—	2	—	3
1 Thess.	—	—	—	—	1	1
2 Thess.	—	—	1	—	—	1
						58

From this table, it is obvious that the root is particularly characteristic of 2 Corinthians and to a lesser extent of Romans and of 1 Corinthians.

The verb *kauchasthai* was frequently translated by Tyndale by the English verb "to rejoice". His example is followed by the Authorized Version in four cases—Rom.5:2; Phil.3:3; Jas.1:9; 4:16. The Revised Standard Version has "rejoice" in Rom.5:2 and 5:11 (where Tyndale and AV use "joy" as a verb), but not in the other three examples. While the rendering "rejoice" may be suitable for a few verses, it is clearly inadequate as a general translation of the verb throughout the New Testament, though joy does play a large part in the idea behind the verb and its cognates.

If the rendering "boast" is felt to be unsuitable in many places, perhaps the word "exult" would convey something of the idea of joy and also the element of boasting that is certainly present in the Greek root.[5] The New English Bible uses "exult" in Rom.5:2 and 11.

Pejorative Connotations

In the New Testament, there is the same double meaning in the root as we found in it in the Old Testament and inter-testamental literature. It is especially in 1 Corinthians that the pejorative connotations appear. Over and over again, Paul uses *kauchasthai* and its cognates to rebuke the boastful pride of certain Christians at Corinth. He insists that "there is no place for *human pride* in the presence of God" (1 Cor.1:29). Party strife has broken out in their midst. Paul argues that they should "never make mere men *a cause for pride*" (1 Cor.3:21). Church members were even condoning a case of flagrant sexual immorality. Paul states categorically: "Your *self-satisfaction* ill becomes you" (1 Cor.5:6).

Paul goes a stage further than previous writers in the process of distinguishing between two types of boasting. He insists that even within the more strictly religious connotation of the root, glorying may be a bad thing. In fact, it has to be dropped entirely, in certain circumstances at least, as a fundamentally irreligious attitude. "What room then is left for *human pride*?" he imagines a pious Jew asking him in his letter to the Romans. He retorts, "It is excluded" (Rom.3:27).

This insistence upon the incongruity of any boasting before God is an important corollary of Paul's doctrine of justification by grace through faith. Mere works of the law are of no profit to anyone. "What, then, are we to say about Abraham, our ancestor in the natural line?" continues the imaginary Jewish interlocutor. Paul maintains his position: "If Abraham was justified by anything he had done, then he has *a ground for pride*. But he has no such ground before God" (Rom.4:2). Earlier in the same letter, Paul has attacked the Jews for relying upon the law and for boasting of their relation to God. In spite of all their "pride in the law", Jews have brought disrepute upon themselves and dishonour upon God by failing to keep the precepts of the very law in which they take pride (Rom.2:17,23).[6]

The attack upon any theory of justification by works recurs with renewed vigour in the letter to the Ephesians. "For it is by his grace you are saved, through trusting him ... There is nothing for anyone to *boast of*" (Eph.2:8f.).

Elsewhere in the New Testament, warnings against vain self-glory appear only in the letter of James. The author has much to say about the evils connected with the tongue. He insists upon good works as the necessary outcome of Christian faith. Boasting, therefore, is excluded since real spiritual wisdom leads to humility (see Jas.3:13f.; 4:16).

Justifiable Boasting

In the vast majority of instances of the verb *kauchasthai* and its cognates in Paul, boasting is regarded as something justifiable provided the object boasted in is a proper one. In Judaism, the religious man had placed his confidence in his own moral and religious achievements (cf. Lk.18:11). In Paul's view as a Christian, however, joyful reliance had to be placed only upon Jesus Christ and his cross. Even Paul's joy in his converts and their pride in him were secondary to, or within the sphere of, their boasting in Jesus Christ (see Phil.1:26).

This issue had been raised with peculiar poignancy amongst the Galatian Christians on account of the fact that certain Judaizers had been at work in their area. In contrast to Jewish pride in circumcision, Paul asserted his joyful boasting in the cross of Jesus Christ (Gal.6:13f., cf. Phil.3:2f.). As a result of this justification by God's grace through faith, "we joy in God through our Lord Jesus Christ, by whom we have now received the atonement" (Rom.5:11—AV; cf. 1 Cor.1:31; 2 Cor.10:15).

As a direct inference from his glorious exultation in God, Paul felt justified in boasting of his work for God (see Rom.15:17; 2 Cor.1:12). He took great pride in his converts to the faith (2 Cor.7:4,14; 10:16-18; Phil.2:16; 1 Thess.2:19). He also felt that every Christian should be able to rejoice in his achievements in Christian service (Gal.6:4).

An eschatological element is introduced into Paul's boasting in certain passages of his correspondence. The Thessalonian Christians are to be his "joy (*chara*—see Chapter One) or crown of *pride*" at the parousia of Christ (1 Thess.2:19). The faith of Christians at Philippi will be his *pride* on that day (Phil.2:16). The same thing will be true in the case of his converts at Corinth (2 Cor.1:14). On account of this future exultation, Paul felt able to rejoice even in his sufferings (Rom.5:3).

In the solitary occurrence of the root in the letter to the Hebrews, it is also connected with the Christian hope. We belong to Christ's household "if only we are fearless and keep our hope high" (Heb.3:6—literally, "... keep the *pride* of our hope").

Even though James realized that much boasting is wrong (Jas.4:16), he nevertheless insisted that all Christians should be able to boast of their common possession of the Gospel of Jesus Christ. Rich and poor are alike in this, as they are also face to face with death (Jas.1:9-11). The latter part of this passage is echoed in Gray's *Elegy written in a Country Church-Yard*:

> The boast of heraldry, the pomp of power,
>   And all that beauty, all that wealth e'er gave
> Awaits alike th' inevitable hour:—
>   The paths of glory lead but to the grave.

In the Letter of James, as in the letters of Paul, we are taken one step further. We are shown the only true and profitable ground on which men, rich and poor, can boast. The contrast is drawn and the whole matter is summed up in words of Jeremiah to which Paul alludes twice: "Let not the wise man boast of his wisdom ... but if any man would boast, let him boast of this, that he understands and knows me. For I am the Lord" (Jer.9:23f.; 1 Cor.1:31; 2 Cor.10:1).

8

BLESSEDNESS or HAPPINESS
makarios, makarizein, makarismos

Classical Greek

Makarios, meaning "blessed" or "happy", first appears in Pindar and thereafter occurs mostly in prose writers, though Euripides was very fond of using it. The form used in Homer is *makar;* but this was properly speaking an epithet of the gods. "The blessed ones" (*hoi makares*) lived a life of supreme happiness, free from care and work and death. Ordinary men seldom reached such a state of happiness in the course of their mortal lives. After Homer, the adjective *makar* came to be reserved especially for the dead. "The islands of the blest" appear first in Hesiod as the place where heroes and demi-gods live a life of joy and rest for ever.

The form *makarios* passed into common, everyday language in the fifth century B.C. as a synonym for *eudaimōn*, which meant "happy" or "fortunate". Nevertheless, it was realized that true blessedness belonged only to the gods. In Plato, "the blessed ones" are the more privileged classes—the rich and the better educated people. By means of their wealth, they have been raised up out of the daily cares and distresses by which common people are troubled.

One of the common uses of the adjectives *makar* anα *makarios* from early times was to introduce a beatitude (*makarismos*)—though other adjectives also could be used in this way (*olbios* = "happy"; *trismakarios* = "thrice-blessed"). Such beatitudes reflect the whole Greek philosophy of life in its varied moods and phases. In early times at least, the minds of the ancients were turned towards earthly goods and values, from which they derived their happiness.[1] The *summum bonum* of parents, for example, was the possession of good and beautiful children.[2] The parents and brothers of Nausicaa were 'thrice-blessed" on account of the beauty of their daughter and sister (Homer: Od.6:154). Odysseus was "happy" (*olbios*) on account of having a faithful and virtuous wife in Penelope (Homer: Od.24:192). Yet such was the unhappiness that could be caused by an unfaithful wife that the unmarried man also can think himself blessed: "O *happy* me, in that I fail to take a wife."[3]

Some beatitudes are maxims of more general validity. Praise of marriage and of children as well as of riches and of power could form the subjects of such maxims or gnomic utterances. Since all these things were considered to be among the chief blessings of life, it is by no means surprising that those who were happy in their possession of them were often declared to be blessed. Honour and fame were also considered to be suitable reasons for congratulations. "Blessed (*olbios*) is he who is ever encompassed by good report."[4]

There are also beatitudes within the religious sphere. The pious man is praised over the outer and inner advantages brought to him by his piety in the same way as the wise man is declared to be blessed on account of his knowledge. Those who have been initiated into the mystery religions were considered to be specially fortunate. "O blessed is he who, by happy favour knowing the sacraments of the gods, leads the life of holy service and is inwardly a member of God's company."[5]

Septuagint

Makarios and its cognates occur quite frequently in the Septuagint—the adjective over sixty times and the cognate verb about twenty-four times. The adjective usually refers to persons, but it is never applied to God in the Septuagint as to the gods in Homer. Occasionally, the verb can mean little more than "to praise", but it can also signify "to make happy". Usually, however, the verb (*makarizein*) has the meaning of "to pronounce blessed or happy", as in classical Greek. It is often found in close association with its cognate adjective. "*Blessed* is he who considers the poor! ... he is *called blessed* in the land" (Ps.41:1f.—RSV). "I can think of nine men I *count happy* ... *happy* the husband of a sensible wife ... the man whose tongue never betrays him ...! *Happy* the man who has found a friend, and the speaker who has an attentive audience!" (Sir.25:7-9)

An echo of Solon's conversation with Croesus can be seen in this warning, "*Call* no man *happy* before he dies" (Sir.11:28) and in the more positive parallel in the Wisdom of Solomon: "*He says* that the just die *happy*" (Wisdom 2:16).

The beatitudes of the Septuagint are found predominantly in the Book of Psalms and in the wisdom literature (especially in Proverbs and in Ben Sirach). They reflect the wishes and the ideals of the ancient Hebrews and are both secular and religious in nature.

As in classical Greek, there are instances where earthly goods and values are the reasons for the pronouncements of blessing; as, for example, when the marriage relationship is extolled. When the Queen of Sheba came to visit King Solomon, she found that his wisdom and his prosperity were even greater than she had been told. She exclaimed: "*Happy* are your wives, *happy* these courtiers of yours who wait on you every day and hear your wisdom!" (1 Kings 10:8 = 2 Chron.9:7) Again, Ben Sirach comments upon the happiness of the husband of a good wife (Sir.26:1; cf. Sir 25:8).

The evils caused by the slanderous tongue call forth a beatitude from Ben Sirach on "the man who is sheltered from its onslaught" (Sir.28:19) and another beatitude on the man who keeps his own tongue in control: "*Happy* the man who has never let slip a careless word, who has never felt the sting of remorse!" (Sir.14:1)

In keeping with the whole character of the wisdom literature, there are several beatitudes in which the possession of wisdom is given as the cause of the declaration of blessedness. "*Happy* he who has found wisdom, and the man who has acquired understanding" (Prov.3:13) and "Happy the man who fixes his thoughts on wisdom and uses his brains to think, the man who contemplates her ways and ponders her secrets" (Sir.14:20).

Most of the beatitudes in the Psalter, as well as a few in other parts of the Septuagint, are more specifically religious in their content. This type can be divided into those which refer to the nation and those which refer to individuals. Of the former, the first to be encountered in the Old Testament is Moses' blessing before his death: "*Happy* are you, people of Israel, peerless, set free; the Lord is the shield that guards you ..." (Deut.33:29). The psalmist speaks in the same vein: "*Happy* is the nation whose God is the Lord, the people he has chosen for his own possession" (Ps.33:12; cf. Ps.144:15). According to Baruch, the happiness of the nation consists in knowing "what is pleasing to God" (Bar.4:4).

In beatitudes on individuals, psalmists show clearly that the only true foundation for personal happiness lies in faith and trust in God and in meditation upon God's law. The first psalm gives a picture of the happy man "who does not take the wicked for his guide, nor walk the road that sinners tread ... the law of the Lord is his delight ..." (Ps.1:1f.; Cf. Ps.112:1; Ps.119:1). Similarly happy are "the man whose disobedience is forgiven, whose sin is put away" (Ps.32:1), "a man when the Lord lays no guilt to his account" (Ps.32:2), and "the man whom thou dost instruct, O Lord, and teach out of thy law" (Ps.94:12; cf. Job 5:17).

The psalmists also express the joy of worship by means of beatitudes. "Happy is the man of thy choice, whom thou dost bring to dwell in thy courts" (Ps.65:4). "Happy are those who dwell in thy house; they never cease from praising thee" (Ps.84:4; cf. Ps.89:15; Is.30:18).

Only once in the course of the psalms is an alien note struck in a beatitude, when the psalmist praises those who will take vengeance upon Babylon for her treatment of the people of Israel: "... *happy* the man who repays you for all that you did to us! *Happy* is he who shall seize your children and dash them against the rock" (Ps.137:8f.). This falls far short of the spirit of him who said: "Love your enemies and pray for your persecutors" (Mt.5:44).

New Testament

The root is found fifty-five times in the New Testament. In almost every case, it has a strictly religious connotation. It signifies the joy that belongs to the person who shares in the salvation of the kingdom of God. The adjective (*makarios*) occurs fifty times, including thirty-two times in the Gospels and Acts (of which only four are not on the lips of Jesus—Lk.1:45; 11:27; 14:15; Acts 26:2) and four times in Paul's letters. The noun (*makarismos*) appears three times in Paul (Rom.4:6-9; Gal.4:15). The verb (*makarizein*) is found twice (Lk.1:48; Jas.5:11).

	Adjective	*Noun*	*Verb*
Matthew	13	—	—
Luke	15	—	1
John	2	—	—
Acts	2	—	—
Paul	4	3	—
Pastorals	3	—	—
James	2	—	1
1 Peter	2	—	—
Revelation	7	—	—

In the majority of these instances, the adjective is found as the introductory word to a beatitude. The formula that is used so frequently in classical Greek and in the Septuagint (*makarios hostis*—the adjective followed by the relative pronoun) occurs only occasionally (see Lk.14:15; cf. Mt.11:6 = Lk.7:23). Instead, the adjective is usually followed by the article with a substantive. Then the ground or proof of the beatitude often comes in an adverbial clause introduced by "for" or "because". The predominance of these beatitudes in Matthew and Luke and in the Book of Revelation can be explained by the fact that, in the New Testament, they belong not to the literature of Wisdom, as in the Septuagint, but to the eschatological announcement of the kingdom of God.[6]

Mary, the mother of Jesus, is twice pronounced blessed in Luke's Gospel, first of all by Elizabeth: "How *happy* is she who has had faith that the Lord's promise would be fulfilled!" (Lk.1:45) The subordinate clause introduced by the Greek word *hoti* could equally well be translated: "for (or because) the

Lord's promise will be fulfilled'' (cf. AV, RV, RSV mg). Then it would state "the reason why the belief is blessed and not the contents of the belief. There is no need to state what Mary believed. Elizabeth adds her faith to Mary's, and declares that, amazing as the promise is, it will assuredly be fulfilled.''[7] This rendering of the Greek would fit in with the other beatitudes, where the subordinate clause most certainly gives the reason or proof.

Later on in Luke's Gospel, Mary is blessed by a woman in the crowd listening to Jesus' words (Lk.11:27). Jesus rebuked this rather coarse reference to his mother not by denying her happiness but by asserting the superior felicity of his true disciples (Lk.11:28). "Physical relationship to the Master is not the highest relationship. Most blessed are they who listen to the word of God, which he teaches, and perform it ...''[8] In contrast to this beatitude on Mary, Jesus suggested on the way to Calvary that the time would come when childless women would be congratulated rather than despised (Lk.23:29).

Both in Matthew and in Luke, the beatitudes found at the beginning of the great sermon of Jesus (Mt.5:3-12; Lk.6:20-23) are addressed to the disciples. In Matthew, there are nine in all. Four of these nine correspond to those in Luke, the stark simplicity of whose words is probably more original.[9] In Luke's Sermon on the Plain, the beatitudes speak to men in certain earthly circumstances—the poor, the hungry, the weeping, and the hated. Jesus promises such people eschatological satisfaction. To the poor belongs the kingdom of God (Lk.6:20), the hungry shall be satisfied (Lk.6:21), those who weep now shall laugh hereafter (Lk.6:21; cf. Mt.5:4), and those who are hated and insulted for Christ's sake have a rich reward waiting them (Lk.6:22f.; cf. Mt.5:11f.). It is not that poverty, hunger, weeping and insults are in themselves qualifications for salvation. "The beatitudes are addressed to disciples, to those who are ready to be persecuted for the sake of the Son of man.''[10]

In Matthew, the earthly circumstances pronounced blessed by Jesus in Luke appear to have been spiritualized. Stress is laid on the fact that right behaviour and right attitudes of mind will be rewarded hereafter. Yet there is no fundamental distinction between the types of people pronounced happy in the two sermons. The rewards held out by Jesus in Luke's Gospel would be considered of value only by the pious. Furthermore, according to Jewish interpretation, "the poor", "the hungry", "the weeping", and "the hated" were those godly people who longed for the triumph of God and who had to face hardships in the world on account of their faith. The contrast between their present circumstances and the future, according to Jesus, is as great as the difference between poverty and riches, hunger and satisfaction, sorrow and joy. Yet even in this world, such persons have compensations and can be called happy.

The extra beatitudes in the Sermon on the Mount are those on those of a gentle spirit (Mt.5:5—"the meek" in AV), those who show mercy (Mt.5:7—"the merciful" in AV), those whose hearts are pure (Mt.5:8), the peacemakers (Mt.5:9), and those who have suffered persecution for the cause of right (Mt.5:10). These five were probably derived by the evangelist from his own special source (labelled M by scholars) as distinct from Q, the source also used by Luke. The fifth (Mt.5:10) seems to be a doublet of the final one in both Matthew and Luke (Mt.5:11f. = Lk.6:22f.). It can therefore be considered the M version of this final beatitude in Q. The first four of the beatitudes peculiar to Matthew were typical Jewish attitudes of piety. They can all be paralleled in the Old Testament or in rabbinic literature.[11]

It is the M version of the beatitude on the persecuted (Mt. 5:10) that seems to be echoed in 1 Peter, where the author reckons with the possibility of suffering for his readers (1 Pet. 3:14). Both the M version and the Q version of this beatitude (Mt.5:10; Mt.5:11f. = Lk.6:22f.) could lie behind Peter's second beatitude (1 Pet.4:14). The Letter of James also contains a beatitude concerning persecution (Jas.1:12).

Matthew has four beatitudes in addition to those in the Sermon on the Mount; and three of them are paralleled in Luke (Mt.11:6 = Lk.7:23; Mt.13:16 = Lk.10:23; Mt.16:17 (M); Mt.24:46 = Lk.12:43; cf. Lk.12:37f. and Rev.16:15). In the case of the second of these, Luke's version seems more original: "*Happy* the eyes that see what you are seeing!" (Lk.10:23) The joy of the disciples consists not so much in the fact that their eyes are open, as in Matthew, but that they are experiencing the coming of the messianic age. In their vision of the realization of Jewish eschatology, the disciples have an advantage over the prophets and kings of old, who desired to see these things.

Luke records how the table-talk of Jesus in the house of a leading Pharisee called forth a pious remark from one of his fellow-guests: *"Happy* the man who shall sit at the feast in the kingdom of God!"* (Lk.14:15) This is one of the few Gospel beatitudes not on the lips of Jesus (cf. Lk.1:45; 11:27). Jesus did not deny the truth of this reflection, but he challenged the sincerity of the speaker by relating the parable of the great feast from which the invited guests absented themselves with trifling excuses (Lk.14:16-24).

In the Acts of the Apostles, Luke records a beatitude of Jesus quoted by Paul in his speech to the Ephesian elders: "It is more *blessed* to give than to receive" (Acts 20:35—RSV). So Jesus taught that the kind of life which seeks to give and to serve rather than to get earns a reward both here and hereafter.

The Fourth Gospel contains two beatitudes—"the beatitude of ministry" (Jn.13:17) and "the beatitude of faith" (Jn. 20:29).[12] In the first, Jesus praised the person who works his Christian beliefs into the very texture of his life and who reaches out to others in Christian service—an idea taken up by James in his letter (Jas.1:27). In the second, Jesus praises those future disciples of his who, unlike Thomas, will believe in him without having seen him.

Paul has few beatitudes of his own in his letters (see Rom.4:7f.; 14:22; 1 Cor.7:40); but there are seven in the Book of Revelation. The first and the sixth of these frame the whole vision that was granted to the writer: *"Happy* is the man who reads, and happy those who listen to the words of this prophecy and heed what is written in it ... *Happy* is the man who heeds the words of prophecy contained in this book!" (Rev.1:3; 22:7) In the course of his vision, John hears a voice from heaven declaring the happiness of those who die as martyrs in the final struggle between the world and the Church: *"Happy* are the dead who die in the faith of Christ from now on!" These words were confirmed by the Spirit, who said: "Happy indeed are they; let them rest from their labours; for they take with them the record of their deeds" (Rev.14:13).[13] The imminence and the unexpectedness of the second coming of Christ lead to the proclamation of the beatitude on Christians who remain faithful during their life on earth (Rev.16:15). Similarly *happy* are "those who are invited to the wedding-supper of the Lamb"

(Rev.19:9), "the man who shares in this first resurrection" (Rev.20:6), and, finally, "those who wash their robes clean! They will have the right to the tree of life and will enter by the gates of the city" (Rev.22:14).[14]

9

LEAPING FOR JOY
skirtan

Classical Greek

This verb means "to spring", "to leap", or "to bound". It is
used in classical Greek both of animals and of human beings.
Homer, for example, gives us a lovely picture of the playfulness
of young foals. "In their frolics on land they could *run across* a
field of corn, brushing the highest ears, and do no harm to it"
(*Iliad* 20:226f.). Theocritus used the verb of the leaping of
goats. Euripides tells us how the Bacchae, the female votaries of
the god Dionysus whom Pentheus rashly imprisoned at Thebes,
broke out of their chains and *"bounded away* to the meadows,
calling upon their god Bromios" (446). The verb seems,
therefore, to have connoted a light, skipping movement. This
was the outward manifestation of a merry, joyful feeling—
whether that feeling was natural as in the case of young animals
or brought about by artificial means as in the case of enthusiastic initiates into the mystic cult of Dionysus, the god of wine.
"Enthusiastic" means literally "having the god inside one"—
so "possessed by the god"—in this case, the god of wine.

Septuagint

There are seven appearances of the word in the Septuagint. The first is unique. It describes how the unborn Jacob and Esau "moved" in their mother's womb. The Hebrew text is translated: "The children pressed hard on each other (struggled together—AV, RSV) in her womb" (Gen.25:22). This was interpreted to Rebecca as a sign that her two sons would found nations which would struggle against each other and that the elder would serve the younger (Gen.25:23). In the Septuagint, however, the verb *skirtan* may be a straightforward reference to the natural movement of unborn babies regarded as being expressive of joy in living. It may be that the Septuagint was the first to use the term in this way.[1]

Elsewhere in the Septuagint, the verb is used of animals or in metaphorical association with animals. Mountains "*skip* like rams" and hills "like young sheep" (Ps.114:4). Israel's enemies, the Babylonians, "*run free* like a heifer after threshing" (Jer.50:11 = Jer.27:11 in LXX). One of the sounds that paralysed people with fear was "the racing of creatures *as they bound along* unseen" (Wisdom 17:19). On the day of the Lord, "you shall *break loose* like calves released from the stall" (Mal.4:2).

New Testament

In the New Testament, the verb occurs only three times and is peculiar to Luke's Gospel. It is used twice in quick succession in chapter one in connection with John the Baptist, who, even before his birth, rejoiced on account of the imminent arrival of the Messiah. Mary, the mother-to-be of Jesus, went to visit Elizabeth. "And when Elizabeth heard Mary's greeting, the baby *stirred* in her womb" (Lk.1:41). Elizabeth, in reporting the occurrence to Mary, added a word for "joy" (*agalliasis*—see Chapter One) and thus gave an interpretation to the event: "When your greeting sounded in my ears, the baby in my womb *leapt* for joy" (Lk.1:45). The words spoken by Elizabeth on this occasion are explicitly stated to have been inspired by the Holy Spirit.

In the early part of the seventeenth century, Hugo Grotius, Dutch jurist and theologian, stated that the verb *skirtan* was a medical term denoting the movement of children in the womb, but he cited no examples of this usage.[2] The only other instances of this technical connotation of the term that have been traced in Greek literature are those already quoted above from the Septuagint concerning Jacob and Esau (Gen.25:22f.).

Finally, Luke uses the aorist imperative plural of this verb in his rendering of the final beatitude given by Jesus in the great sermon, where Matthew has the verb *agalliasthai* (Mt.5:12—see Chapter One). When they suffer insults for Christ's sake, the disciples are told to "be glad (*chairein*—see Chapter Ten) and *dance for joy*; for assuredly you have a rich reward in heaven" (Lk.6:23). The eschatological note is evident here as in Malachi. In the present instance, however, the "dancing for joy" is to be done "on that day" when persecution takes place in anticipation of the reward in heaven, and not simply "on the day of the Lord" (Mal.4:2).

Leaping for joy

The element of exuberant joy that is undoubtedly present in this Greek verb on each of its literary appearances can be paralleled in two more modern examples in English.

In his *Pilgrim's Progress*, John Bunyan tells of Christian's experience of forgiveness at the cross. After the burden of sin had rolled from his back, "Christian gave three leaps for joy, and went on singing."

The second example comes from Scotland. John Duncan was Professor of Old Testament at Edinburgh University in the nineteenth century. He was known affectionately to his students as "Rabbi" Duncan. He used to say: "When I knew there was a God, I danced upon the Brig o' Dee with delight."[3]

10

INWARD JOY
chairein, chara

Classical Greek

Chairein is derived from the root *char-*, from which we get not only the noun *chara* (= joy) but also *charis* (= favour, grace). In this chapter, we are concerned mainly with *chairein* and with the cognate noun *chara*, and only in passing with *charis*. The etymological connection between these two nouns suggests, on the face of it, that "favour" or "grace" is something that brings "joy" to people.[1] In Chapter Eleven, we shall study the compound verb *sunchairein*.

The simple verb means "to rejoice", "to be glad", "to be pleased or delighted". It is very common in classical Greek literature from the time of Homer onwards. In the imperative form, either in the singular (*chaire*) or in the plural (*chairete*), it was the usual greeting both at meeting and at parting.

Greek Papyri Letters

The infinitive *chairein* is found very frequently in the papyri in the opening address of letters. The formula is generally the same: "A to B *greeting*." Occasionally we find "many greetings" (*polla chairein*), or "very many *greetings*" (*pleista chairein*), or *"greetings* and good health".

There is even a deed of divorce which opens with such a greeting: "Soulis, grave-digger ... to Senpsais, daughter of Psais and of Tees, grave-digger, ... *greeting*." [2] This deed of divorce dates from A.D. 305/6.

In a few cases, the imperative is found instead; for example, in one of the Oxyrhynchus papyri, which reads: *"Greeting*, my lord Apion."[3] The normal procedure, however, was to use the infinitive.

Septuagint

Both verb and noun occur frequently in the Septuagint—about eighty and forty times respectively.

The epistolary infinitive is used in letters and other documents; as, for example, in the letter sent to the Persian king by officials in Syria, which begins: "To king Darius *greeting*" (1 Esdras 6:7—NEB has "our humble duty" here; cf. 1 Esdras 8:9). In the four books of the Maccabees, there are at least nineteen examples of this infinitive, sometimes with additional good wishes for health and prosperity.

Both verb and noun are found in many other secular connections. In fact, Conzelmann states categorically that *chairein* is intrinsically a secular term.[4] Pleasure on the receipt of news (Gen.45:16; 4 Macc.4:22) or on the arrival of ambassadors of good will (1 Kings 20:13; Is.39:2) or on the meeting of friends or relatives (Ex.4:14) or on the hearing of a proposal about a trade treaty (1 Kings 5:7)—each of these is expressed by means of this verb.

Joy at a wedding (Tobit 11:17) or on winning a victory (2 Macc.15:28) or on receiving permission to wreak vengeance on traitors (3 Macc.7:13,15)—in each of these cases the noun *chara* is used.

Even though *chairein* and *chara* may be intrinsically secular terms, these words are used in many instances in the Septuagint to give expression to joy in a religious context. Sometimes there is a backward glance at deliverances wrought by God on behalf of his people (see 1 Sam.19:5; 1 Kings 8:66; Ps.126:1-3; Joel 2:21); or there may be a calling to mind of blessings from God enjoyed in the present (see Ps.21:6; Joel 2:23).

Religious joy is seen above all in connection with the religious festivals of the Jews. Zechariah, for example, announces that certain fasts "shall become festivals of *joy* and gladness (*euphrosunē*—see Chapter Three) for the house of Judah" (Zech.8:19). Judas Maccabaeus gave orders that the Feast of Dedication should be celebrated each year for eight days "with joy (*euphrosunē*) and *gladness*" (1 Macc.4:59). Similarly, the Feast of Purim was instituted with "*joy* and gladness (*euphrosunē*) to celebrate the deliverance of the Jews from those who had sought to exterminate them throughout the Persian Empire (Esther 8:17).

New Testament

When we turn to the New Testament, we find that it is this root that is the most common expression for joy. It occurs 141 times out of a total of 326 instances of our cognates and synonyms for joy.

	Verb	Compound verb	Noun
Matthew	6	—	6
Mark	2	—	1
Luke	12	3	8
John	9	—	9
Acts	7	—	4
Paul	29	4	21
Pastorals	—	—	1
Hebrews	—	—	4
James	1	—	2
1 Peter	2	—	1
1,2,3 Jn.	4	—	3
Rev.	2	—	—
	74	7	60

From this table, we see that the verb *chairein* appears 74 times while the noun *chara* is found 60 times. In addition, the compound verb *sunchairein*, which we shall be studying in the next chapter, occurs seven times. A cursory glance at this table also reveals that the root is particularly frequent in Paul and in Luke, and that the Fourth Gospel, too, is fond of using it.

Epistolary Infinitive

The infinitive (*chairein*) is found three times at the opening of letters (Acts 15:23; 23:26; Jas.1:1). This was the normal way for a Greek letter to open, as we have seen from the papyri and the Septuagint. Yet of the New Testament letters, only the letter of James opens in this way.

Instead of the usual formula, the Apostle Paul substituted the other cognate noun *charis* (= grace). To this he added a Greek translation of the familiar Semitic form of salutation, *"shalōm"* (Greek: *eirēnē* = peace). Paul used these terms with their full theological connotation—"the grace of God" and "the peace of God". The latter implied the cessation of hostility towards God and the peace of mind following upon such reconciliation, while the former signified the divine love working in redemption and shown forth supremely in the life and death and resurrection of Jesus Christ. The abandonment of the simple greeting (*chairein*) in favour of the noun "grace" (*chara*) not only shows the dominant place of the doctrine of grace in Paul's religious thought. It also points to an intimate connection between the Christian conception of joy and the doctrine of grace. It is on account of the grace of God and all that that implies that we are able to rejoice at all as Christians.

Parallel to the use of the infinitive in letters is its occurrence in 2 John in the sense of an ordinary greeting to someone entering the house as a guest (2 Jn.10f.).

Imperatives

Another use of the infinitive is to be noted in the letter to the Romans: "With the joyful *be joyful*, and mourn with the mourners" (Rom.12:15). Both English imperatives here translate Greek infinitives. This imperatival infinitive was familiar in Greek, especially in laws and maxims. It can be seen even in the papyri.[5]

The imperative proper appears six times in the Gospels in the sense of "Hail!" (Lk.1:28; Mt.26:49; Mt.27:29 = Mk.15:18 = Jn.19:3; Mt.28:9). This use of the imperative of *chairein* as a greeting, like the Latin *salve*, is very common in classical Greek. It could also be used as a farewell greeting on leaving people, like the Latin *vale*. It appears once in this sense in the New Testament at the close of 2 Corinthians: "And now, my friends, *farewell*" (2 Cor.13:11).[6] Bultmann, on the other hand, takes the Greek here as an exhortation to joyfulness and maintains

that ancient letters do not confirm the imperative as a closing
formula of farewell.[7]

Joy and Delight

For the most part, the verb *chairein* is used in the New
Testament to describe an attitude of joy or delight, usually in a
good sense. In a few cases, the rejoicing is inopportune, to say
the least. "Love does not *gloat over* other men's sins" (1
Cor.13:6), wrote Paul in his great hymn on *agapē* (= love); but
this is exactly what the enemies of Jesus did. The chief priests
"were *greatly pleased* (Mk.14:11 = Lk.22:5) when Judas
Iscariot came to them with his offer to betray his Master. When
Pilate sent his Prisoner to Herod and when the latter saw Jesus,
he, too, "was *greatly pleased*" (Lk.23:8). In the Book of
Revelation, we are told that "all men on earth *gloat over*" the
death of the two faithful witnesses (Rev.11:10).

Similarly, Jesus had predicted that his own death would bring
joy to his enemies and sorrow to his disciples, but also that these
emotions would soon be reversed by the turn of events
(Jn.16:20). To press home his point, Jesus used the image of a
woman in labour. Her anguish is turned into joy on the birth of
her child (Jn.16:21). Likewise, the disciples have sorrow at the
prospect of losing their Master. The purpose of the farewell
discourses was to prepare them for that time. They would
eventually have the joy of Jesus within them (Jn.15:11; 17:13;
cf. 1 Jn.1:4).

Joy plays a large part in the Easter story. The women at the
tomb (Mt.28:8) as well as the disciples in the upper room
(Lk.24:41) experienced this emotion when they realized the
truth of the resurrection. Not only so; but when they parted
company with their risen Lord on his ascension, they returned
to the city of Jerusalem "with great *joy*" (Lk.24:52).

Teaching of Jesus

Joy was a supreme characteristic of the teaching of Jesus. So
we find this root not infrequently on his lips in the Gospels. The
shepherd "*is delighted*" over the finding of the missing sheep
(Lk.15:5), "there is *joy* among the angels of God over one
sinner who repents" (Lk.15:10), and the father of the returned

prodigal felt "it was fitting to make merry (*euphrainein*—see Chapter Three) and *be glad*" (Lk.15:32).

The twin parables of the hid treasure and the costly pearl (Mt.13:44-46) are often understood as a summons by Jesus to self-surrender. The emphasis in both, however, is upon the joy of finding something of great value. When a man is overcome by the "sheer joy" of discovering the good news of the Christian gospel, no price is too great to pay. His heart is filled with gladness and the whole aim of his life is the consummation of the divine community.[8] It is of interest that, in the Coptic Gospel of Thomas, these two parables are not found together as double parables. They are logia 109 and 76 respectively. This may mean that originally they were not paired by Jesus and that whoever composed the Gospel of Thomas found them separated in a source (or sources) independent of the canonical Gospels.[9] Nevertheless, the point of each parable seems to be the same. This was realized by the evangelist whom we know as "Matthew"—or perhaps by the compiler of his source M. Even though the words *apo tēs charas autou* ("for sheer joy") appear only in the first of the pair of parables, they clearly apply to the merchant as well as to the man who found buried treasure. There is an interesting parallel to this "sheer joy" in one of Paul's letters, where he refers to the welcome given to the message of the Gospel by his converts at Thessalonica. Their joy was inspired by the Holy Spirit (1 Thess.1:6).

In the parable of the talents, there is a description of the rewards given to the two faithful servants. Each of them doubled the money entrusted to him by their master and so earned his praise. The joy into which they entered was that of fuller service on behalf of their master and added responsibilities (Mt.25:21,23).

Suffering and Eschatology

Both in the teaching of Jesus and in the rest of the New Testament, *chairein* and *chara* are often closely associated with suffering. Jesus warned his disciples that they would be persecuted for his sake. Yet they could accept such hardship "with *gladness* and exultation (*agalliasthai*—see Chapter One)" on account of the reward awaiting them in the future (Mt.5:12; cf. Lk.6:23). The sequel to this is found in the rejoicing of the

apostles after they had been beaten for teaching in the name of
Jesus (Acts 5:41). Paul also could rejoice in his sufferings for
the sake of Christ and for the benefit of the Church (Col.1:24).
His prayer for the Colossian Church members was that they,
too, might have such joy in suffering (Col.1:11).

This note is sounded again in 1 Peter. In addition, there is the
thought that in suffering as a Christian one is actually sharing
the sufferings of Christ (1 Pet.4:13). An eschatological element
is also introduced here—"When his glory is revealed, your *joy*
will be triumphant"—as in the letter to the Hebrews, whose
recipients had *"cheerfully* accepted the seizure of" their
possessions, because they knew that they "possessed something
better and more lasting" (Heb.10:34). So Jesus had endured the
cross on account of "the *joy* that lay ahead of him" (Heb.12:2).
The leaders of the church are exhorted to perform their duties in
remembrance of the day of reckoning. They are to do this
"*joyfully* and not sadly" (Heb.13:17—RSV).

Eschatological hope as the basis of Christian joy had already
been hinted at by Jesus in his speech to the seventy-two on their
joyful return from their mission of evangelism. They were not
to attach too much importance to the subjection of demons.
They were rather to rejoice in the fact that they were enrolled as
citizens of the heavenly kingdom (Lk.10:20). Such a hope
should keep Christians joyful (Rom.12:12; cf. Jn.14:28). The
realization of this hope is described in the song of triumph in the
Book of Revelation: "*Exult* and shout for joy (*agalliasthai*—see
Chapter One) and do him homage, for the wedding-day of the
Lamb has come" (Rev.19:7).

Conclusion

Such are some of the examples of the use of these words in the
New Testament, giving expression to the joy at the heart of the
new religion. Joy in believing the Christian faith (Lk.19:6; Acts
8:8,39; 13:48) is evident throughout. The expansion of
Christianity in the Mediterranean world and the upbuilding of
the church in various communities were attended by joy both in
the towns themselves and in the rest of the Christian church
(see Acts 15:3). Paul was continually rejoicing over his friends
and converts in the various churches (1 Thess.3:9; Col.2:5;
Phil.1:4,18; Rom.16:19).

On several occasions, joy is mentioned in connection with the Holy Spirit (see, e.g., Acts 13:52; 1 Thess.1:6; Rom.14:17); for true Christian joy is inspired by the Spirit of God. In the list of qualities that make up "the harvest of the Spirit", *joy* takes second place after love (*agapē*) and is followed by peace (Gal.5:22).

Chairein and *chara* appear especially where there is mention of the eschatological fulfilment of God's plan of salvation in Jesus Christ. Life in Christ and the hope of glory beyond this present world of time and space both bring this inward state of *joy* to the Christian. It should also be remembered that the whole message of the New Testament is good news of great joy for all people (cf. Lk.2:10).[10] Christianity is a message of joy from beginning to end.

11

SHARED JOY
sunchairein

Classical Greek, Septuagint and Papyri

The primary meaning of this verb is "to rejoice with". In this sense, it is found frequently in classical Greek literature from the fifth century on. The secondary signification of "to wish someone joy", "to congratulate", occurs occasionally in the works of fourth century Attic orators and in the historian Polybius.

The verb appears twice in the Septuagint. After the birth of Isaac, Sarah declares: "God has given me good reason to laugh, and everyone who hears will *laugh* with me" (Gen.21:6—LXX: "rejoice with me"). Then again, in 3 Maccabees, we are told of the congratulations sent by the Jews to King Ptolemy after his victory over Philopater whereby he was encouraged to visit Jerusalem (3 Macc.1:8).

There are a few appearances of the verb in Greek papyri. In the British Museum, a letter is preserved from the 2nd century B.C.. A mother writes to her son congratulating him on learning the Egyptian script: "I rejoiced for you and for myself."[1]

From the third century A.D., there is a letter in which a father writes to his son congratulating him upon his happy marriage.[2]

New Testament

Sunchairein occurs seven times in the New Testament—three times in Luke's Gospel and twice each in 1 Corinthians and in the letter to the Philippians.

Congratulations were received by Elizabeth from her neighbours and relatives on the birth of John the Baptist, as Sarah before her on the birth of Isaac. *"They were as delighted as* she was" on account of "the great favour the Lord had shown her" (Lk.1:58).

Again, in chapter fifteen, when the shepherd had recovered the lost sheep, his delight was so great that he invited his neighbours and friends to celebrate with him: *"Rejoice with me! I have found my lost sheep"* (Lk.15:6). This overflowing joy at the recovery of what had been lost is echoed in the next parable, when the woman had found her missing coin (Lk.15:9). One of the marks of great joy is that it seeks to share itself with other people.

This note of sympathy in rejoicing, as well as in suffering, among the various members of the human body—and by analogy among the various members of the church as the body of Christ—is emphasized by Paul. "If one organ suffers, they all suffer together. If one flourishes, they all *rejoice together"* (1 Cor.12:26). To counteract party disputes and pride over the possession of spiritual gifts, Paul urges that any talents given by God to individuals are meant for the benefit of the whole church. Then he proceeds to emphasize that the finest gift of all is *agapē*—that supreme quality of love that is the mark of God himself (cf. 1 Jn.4:9) and that has "flooded our inmost heart through the Holy Spirit he has given us" (Rom.5:5). One of the characteristics of this *agapē* is that it "does not gloat over (*chairein*—see Chapter Ten) other men's sins, but *delights in* the truth" (1 Cor.13:6).

The imminent prospect of trial and death that faced Paul as he wrote to the Philippians led him to burst forth into sympathetic joy with the church because of the supreme witness that he will thereby be giving for his faith. "I am glad of it, and I *share my gladness* with you all. Rejoice (*chairein*), you no less than I, and let us *share our joy"* (Phil.2:17f.). Thus, sympathy in rejoicing is the note that is struck by *sunchairein* in Philippians as in 1 Corinthians.

Conclusion

The use of this compound verb in the New Testament serves to emphasize one important aspect of Christian joy—and indeed of the Christian religion in general. It must be shared in order to be properly enjoyed. It is not a selfish joy. All true Christianity is missionary in outlook. The joy of the good news of the Gospel of Jesus Christ is meant to be passed on to others. Indeed, "to preserve the joy of religion, the gaiety of our faith and its humanity, we must share it".[3] Karl Barth has made this point as follows: "We can have joy ... only as we give it to others. Like health, joy is also a social matter. There may be cases where a man can be really merry in isolation. But these are exceptional and dangerous ... It certainly gives us ground to suspect the nature of his joy as real joy if he does not desire—'Rejoice with me'—that at least one or some or many others, as representatives of the rest, should share this joy."[4]

A new dimension is given to shared joy within the fellowship of the Christian church; for everything is transformed by *agapē* (love). It is indeed the church alone that can deepen purely social joy and guarantee to it a new and permanent existence, for *agapē*, like faith and hope, "lasts for ever" (1 Cor.13:13).[5]

12

VARIETIES OF JOY

Such is the variety of words for joy found in the New Testament. In certain cases, the usage differs considerably from that in classical Greek. Sometimes the change can be traced through the Septuagint; as, for example, in the case of *agallian* (see Chapter One). This word seems to have been coined for use in biblical Greek, as we have already noted. In other cases, words found infrequently in classical Greek occur frequently in the New Testament; as, for example, the verb *kauchasthai* (see Chapter Seven). The New Testament writers (as also the translators of the Septuagint) were almost a law to themselves as far as their adaptation of words has been concerned. We are reminded of the words of Humpty Dumpty: "When I use a word, it means just what I choose it to mean—neither more nor less."[1] This warns us, too, that words must always be interpreted within their particular contexts. To take a simple example; the fact that *euphrainein* and *euphrosunē* are sometimes associated with festive joy in the Septuagint and in the intertestamental literature does not mean that, in every instance in the New Testament, they must have this association with a meal or festival.

There are, of course, New Testament words for joy which show obvious resemblances to their counterparts in classical

	Matt.	Mk.	Lk.	Jn.	Acts	Paul	Pastorals	Heb.	1-3 Jn.	1 Pet.	2 Pet.	Jas.	Jude	Rev.
Exultant Joy (agallian/agalliasis)	1	-	4	2	3	-	-	1	-	3	-	-	1	1
Optimism (euthumein/euthumos)	-	-	-	-	4	-	-	-	-	-	-	1	-	-
Gladness (euphrainein/euphrosunē)	-	-	6	-	4	3	-	-	-	-	-	-	-	3
Pleasure (hēdonē/hēdus/hēdeōs)	-	2	1	-	-	3	1	-	-	-	1	2	-	-
Courage (tharsein/tharrein/tharsos)	3	2	-	1	2	5	-	1	-	-	-	-	-	-
Hilarity (hilaros/hilarotēs)	-	-	-	-	-	2	-	-	-	-	-	-	-	-
Boasting (kauchasthai/kauchēma/kauchēsis)	-	-	-	-	-	58	-	1	-	-	5	-	-	7
Blessedness (makarios/makarizein/makarismos)	13	-	16	2	2	7	3	-	-	2	-	3	-	7
Leaping for Joy (skirtan)	-	-	3	-	-	-	-	-	-	-	-	-	-	-
Inward Joy (chairein/chara)	12	3	20	18	11	50	1	4	7	3	-	3	-	2
Shared Joy (sunchairein)	-	-	3	-	-	4	-	-	-	-	-	-	-	-
	29	7	53	23	26	132	5	7	7	8	1	14	1	13

Greek—even though some kind of development can be traced. This is true, for example, of *makarios* (see Chapter Eight). In this case, we can see realized or inaugurated eschatology[2] at work. The happiness that in ancient times was reserved for the gods, for the dead and for specially favoured mortals during their lifetime, is now available to men and women even in this present life, though its full realization is still to come in the heavenly kingdom.

The spread of these cognates and synonyms for joy over the various books of the New Testament is also of interest, as we see from the accompanying table. The 53 occurrences of these words in Luke's Gospel indicate that his is "The Gospel of Joy". The Apostle Paul is also fond of using these words. In fact, every New Testament writer has something to say about joy, in one or more of its varieties. Each author has some contribution to make towards our understanding of the Christian conception of joy. Much, therefore, can be gained by studying each of them in turn in order to discover how he uses these words.

As we do this in Part Two, we shall discover, as James Denney put it, that "there is not in the New Testament from beginning to end, in the record of the original and genuine Christian life, a single word of despondency or gloom. It is the most buoyant, exhilarating, and joyful book in the world."[3]

Part Two
OUR HERITAGE OF JOY

13

THE MAN OF JOY — JESUS

Jesus was indeed "a man of sorrows and acquainted with grief" (Is.53:3); for his life was one of many sorrows and disappointments. To him belonged the sorrow of sympathy with sufferers, the sorrow of rejection by those whom he loved, the sorrow of being hated by those whom he had come to save. While we are never told that Jesus laughed or smiled, we are twice shown him weeping—at the tomb of Lazarus (Jn.11:35) and on the way up to Jerusalem on Palm Sunday (Lk.19:41). Mark tells us that on two separate occasions Jesus sighed. There was the sigh of compassion at the sight of a man who was deaf and dumb (Mk. 7:34). There was also the sigh of indignation at the request of the Pharisees for a sign from heaven (Mk.8:12).

The sorrow of Jesus was particularly evident during the last week of his earthly life. The prospect of death by crucifixion filled him with foreboding as he deliberated upon what he should do (Jn.12:27). At the Last Supper, he was again troubled in spirit as he foretold the betrayal by one of his disciples (Jn.13:21). In the Garden of Gethsemane, horror and dismay came over him and his heart was ready to break with grief (Mk.14:34).

Nevertheless, there was in the life and teaching of Jesus an abounding joy that surpassed and transformed all the sufferings and sorrows he had to bear. If he can justly be characterised as "a man of sorrows and acquainted with grief", he can with equal truth be described as "the man of joy". Shining right through his life—even at its darkest·moments—there was a note of radiance and triumphant joy. Optimism and joyful trust in his heavenly Father were the keynotes of his life and ministry.

Joy was thus an ever-present reality in the life and work of Jesus. Wherever he went in Galilee, he left some mark of cheerfulness and hope in the lives of the common people. The atmosphere of sheer exuberance that surrounded his public ministry has been finely described by Renan: "He traversed Galilee in the midst of a continual feast. ... His entering a house was considered a joy and a blessing. He stopped in the villages and the large farms, where he received an eager hospitality. ... The mothers ... brought him their children in order that he might touch them. Women came to pour oil upon his head, and perfume on his feet."[1] The very fact that Jesus did attract such people to himself shows that he cannot have been forbidding in his manner. It suggests that the "man of sorrows" conception of his personality has been overrated in the past. Had he been a gloomy individual and a kill-joy, he would not have had such an appeal to common people and to children.

Even though the joy of Jesus shines through the Gospel records, it is but seldom that the evangelists expressly attribute this emotion to our Lord. In spite of the fact that words for joy of some kind or other occur one hundred and twelve times in the four Gospels, it is only on three of these occasions that Jesus himself is the subject. There is a fourth reference to the joy of Jesus in the New Testament—in the letter to the Hebrews. As we examine these four passages, we discover the secret that lay behind his unique personality of joy.

Luke's Gospel

Luke tells us that when the seventy-two returned from their successful mission of evangelism, they were filled with joy at what they had accomplished in the name of Jesus (Lk.10:17). Jesus warned them not to attach too much importance to such miraculous powers of exorcism. They should rather rejoice in the fact that they are reckoned among God's people. Then follows the record of Jesus' own experience of exultation (Lk.

10:21). According to Luke, the joy of Jesus on this occasion was inspired by the Holy Spirit. From beginning to end, his life was one of divine inspiration. Having been conceived by the Holy Spirit (Lk.1:35), he was born in the fulness of time. In his early years, he gave evidence of the divine power behind his life in that "he advanced in wisdom and in favour with God and men" (Lk.2:52). At his baptism in the River Jordan, "the Holy Spirit descended on him in bodily form like a dove" (Lk.3:22), and thereafter he was "for forty days led by the Spirit up and down the wilderness and tempted by the devil" (Lk.4:1f.). In his ministry of healing and preaching "the Spirit of the Lord" was upon him (Lk.4:18). Such was the secret of his whole life upon earth. Such also was to be the motive power behind the lives of the disciples after his ascension (Lk.24:49). When we take all this into account, we can understand how Luke could think of the joy of Jesus on the return of the seventy-two as being inspired by the Holy Spirit.

The reason for Christ's exultation of spirit was quite different from the motive behind the joy of the returned missionaries. It was not the success of the mission as such that moved him to exult. Rather was it the additional evidence provided of the method of revelation chosen by God that thrilled his heart (Lk.10:21). The knowledge of God was no longer the preserve of a select few—such as the rabbis, who were specially trained to understand it. It was open to simple-hearted people, such as those to whom the seventy-two had been sent. In other words, Jesus rejoiced that religion as a first-hand experience of the divine by mankind required no elaborate instruction, but simple trust and confidence in God as heavenly Father.[2]

The Fourth Gospel

The joy of Jesus was evident even on the night of his betrayal.[3] In the course of his farewell speech, he said: "I have spoken thus to you, so that my joy may be in you, and your joy complete" (Jn.15:11). In other words, the joy that Jesus experienced could be part of the experience of his disciples also.

This joy of Jesus was the joy of unbroken fellowship with the Father. The supreme title that Jesus gave to God was "Father". His whole life upon earth was one of communion with his heavenly Father. This fellowship with God the Father is part of the secret of Christian joy, as illustrated in an incident from the life of Edward Irving.[4] On the hills near Annan, he once met a shepherd with a joyless look. The great preacher said to him quietly, "Do you know the Father?" Some years afterwards, in the streets of Annan, the shepherd came up to him and said, "I know the Father now, sir." The shepherd had passed out of a life of isolation into the great fellowship of God.

There was another secret of the joy of Jesus—his whole-hearted obedience to the will of God. "My aim," he said on one occasion, "is not my own will, but the will of him who sent me" (Jn.5:30). In the upper room he could say: "I have heeded my Father's commands" (Jn.15:10). This obedience was given supreme expression in his submission to death upon the cross. "Bearing the human likeness, revealed in human shape, he humbled himself, and in obedience accepted even death—death on a cross" (Phil.2:8). Because of this loyalty to the Father's will, Jesus remained within God's love (Jn.15:10). This love of the Father for the Son constituted the second strand in their mutual relationship. Both together—obedience and love—comprised their unity of spirit in one divine fellowship and brought into being the joy which Jesus claimed as his own.

Such also was the joy that could be shared by the disciples. The purpose of Jesus' teaching was that they should be able to participate in this experience of fellowship with him and with the Father. But the conditions required from them were identical with those fulfilled by himself—obedience and love. In so far as they remained in his love and obeyed his commandments, they would share in his joy—the joy of divine fellowship. Yet their experience of the love of Jesus for them was dependent upon themselves. It was conditional upon their obedience to him, exactly as his own experience of the divine love was the outcome of his obedience to the Father's will (Jn.15:10).

The nature of the commands of Jesus to his disciples is described in part in the following verse (Jn.15:11). A new standard was given to them for their brotherly love. It must be a love that pours itself out in sacrifice if it is to be like the love of Jesus for them (Jn.15:11).

The supreme necessity of love—the Greek word is *agapē*—becomes clear. Without it, we cannot expect to participate in that communion with the Father and with the Son that is the

prerequisite of sharing in the joy of Jesus—the joy of unbroken
fellowship with the Father. The joy of Jesus can remain with us
and our joy can be complete only as we continue daily in the
divine fellowship and obey Christ's commandment: "Love one
another" (Jn.15:17).

All this is borne out further by the second reference that Jesus
made to his joy in the course of the farewell discourses. In the
high-priestly prayer, Jesus prayed aloud for his disciples in
order that they might overhear his intercessions for them and
rejoice (Jn.17:13). Here again the joy of Jesus is clearly that of
union with the Father. Though Jesus himself, in perpetual
communion with the Father, was not obliged to rely on prayer
as a formal observance, the prayers that he spoke aloud showed
the disciples the fellowship he enjoyed with the Father and
provided a pattern for the fellowship with the Father that his
disciples would subsequently enjoy. Prayer helped, therefore, to
convey to them his joy—the joy of unsparing obedience to and
unbroken communion with the Father.

The Letter to the Hebrews

The unknown author of the letter to the Hebrews summoned
his readers to perseverance in the Christian life by directing
them to "Jesus who, for the sake of the joy that lay ahead
of him, endured the cross, making light of its disgrace, and
has taken his seat at the right hand of the throne of God"
(Heb.12:2).

There is a two-fold aspect of joy here. There is, first of all, the
unselfish joy of Christ's vicarious suffering—the delight taken
by Jesus in his work of atonement performed by "tasting death
for us all" (Heb.2:9). Jesus was able to rejoice because he knew
that he would redeem his people from sin, from fear and from
death. It was for this reason that he "endured the cross, making
light of its disgrace, and has taken his seat at the right hand of
the throne of God". The ascension and the exaltation of Christ
were necessary for the completion of the work of redemption
and atonement. They are not purely selfish rewards given to him
"because he suffered death" (Heb.2:9).

In addition to this joy of self-sacrificing service, there is in
this passage in Hebrews eschatological joy. The hope of
glory—the prospect of resuming that position of honour and

power that had been his before the incarnation—this also was part of "the joy that lay ahead of him".

This eschatological element was not merely the unselfish joy of completing the work of atonement and of carrying on his ministry of intercession by means of his exaltation to the right hand of the throne of God. It also involved his own personal joy as the reward of faithful service upon earth and of obedience to the Father's will even to death. It is this aspect that the author of Hebrews is emphasising. In the previous chapter, he has been enumerating examples of Old Testament characters who endured trials in this world as "strangers or passing travellers on earth". They were "looking for a country of their own ... longing for a better country—I mean, the heavenly one" (Heb.11:13-16). Now Jesus himself is taken as the supreme example of such endurance. He can be an inspiration to all who have to bear hardship as his followers. In the midst of persecution and of dangers of one kind and another, Christians can remain faithful by keeping firmly before them the eschatological hope, as did Jesus himself.

The Joy of Jesus

From these four references to the joy of Jesus, we can come to certain conclusions. With Christ, as with Paul later, joy was part of "the fruit of the Spirit" (Gal.5:22). It resulted from knowledge of the fact that ordinary people could have fellowship with God and trust in him as their heavenly Father. The joy of Jesus came through obedience to the Father's will and through mutual love between the Father and the Son. It was the joy of self-sacrificing service. Jesus endured the trials of life by means of the divine joy that was set before him and because of the certain hope that was his of glory to come beyond death.

14

THE GOSPEL OF JOY AND ITS SEQUEL —
LUKE AND ACTS

It is St Luke's Gospel that is *par excellence* "the Gospel of Joy". Of the 326 instances of words for joy in the New Testament, 53 occur within these 24 chapters. In addition, words for joy appear 26 times in the Acts of the Apostles. Thus, 24% of the New Testament vocabulary for joy is contained within the writings of Luke, the beloved physician and travelling companion of the Apostle Paul. As Adolf Harnack wrote, "What a trumpet-note of joy, courage, and triumph sounds through the whole Lukan history, from the first to the last pages! *Vexilla regis prodeunt!*"[1] This joyful aspect of the message of Jesus Christ and its other elements of universal appeal are set forth by Luke with such matchless literary art that his gospel was declared by Ernest Renan to be "the most beautiful book in the world".

The Prelude to the Gospel

The note of joy is sounded no less than ten times in the very first chapter of Luke's Gospel in connection with the prophecies about the birth of Jesus and the birth of John the Baptist. As Zechariah was performing his duties as priest in the Temple, he was told that he and Elizabeth would have a son. "Your heart will thrill with joy and many will be glad that he was born"

(Lk.1:14). Mary was addressed as "most favoured one" by the angel Gabriel, who foretold the birth of Jesus: "Greetings, most favoured one! The Lord is with you" (Lk.1:28). Since the grace of God had come upon her in a unique way, she had special qualifications for being greeted with joy both by the angel and by Elizabeth's unborn baby (Lk.1:44). In the first of these two cases (Lk.1:28), there is a play on words in Greek, since the word for "grace" (*chara*) incorporated into the verbal adjective "most favoured one" (*kecharitōmenē*) is derived from the same root (*char*) as is the Greek word for "joy" (*chara*) found here in the infinitive form (*chairein*) used as a greeting.[2]

We learn in this opening chapter of Luke's Gospel that Mary, on being told of the destiny in store for her, went in haste to visit her kinswoman, Elizabeth, and confided in her. Her confidence was not misplaced. Whatever others might think and say, Elizabeth was prepared to believe the best of Mary. With keen intuition—"filled with the Holy Spirit" (Lk.1:41)—she greeted her as "blessed" (Lk.1:45). The congratulations bestowed upon her by Elizabeth provoked Mary to break out into humble thanksgiving to God in what is now known as the Magnificat—from the introductory word in the Latin Vulgate. This is the first of four hymns recorded by Luke in his opening chapters—the others being the Benedictus (Lk.1:68-79), the Gloria (Lk.2:14), and the Nunc Dimittis (Lk.2:29-32).

The Magnificat appears to have been a hymn already in existence which Mary adapted—perhaps with the alteration of a word here and there—to suit her own circumstances. Its various phrases can be paralleled from the Old Testament, particularly from Hannah's prayer of thanksgiving on the birth of Samuel (1 Sam.2:1-10). After the opening expression of joyful thanksgiving, Mary passes on quickly to give the reason for her rejoicing—the promise of the birth of a son. The strains of joy rise as she reflects upon the mercy of God both towards herself and towards the nation of Israel. The hymn thus comprises two stanzas, both of which lead up to the idea of "mercy". In the first stanza, the singer rejoices in patient humility and thanksgiving over God's goodness to herself. In the second stanza, she breaks into a triumphant *fortissimo* of praise on account of the mighty acts of God in scattering the proud overlords of Palestine and in raising up the downtrodden in accordance with his promises to Abraham. So the keyword of the Magnificat is "mercy"—God's goodness both to the individual and to the nation of Israel.

The individual aspect of God's mercy occurs immediately after the Magnificat when Elizabeth's neighbours and relatives "were as delighted as she was" over the birth of John the Baptist (Lk.1:58).

The comprehensive aspect of God's mercy in Jesus Christ appears in chapter two, where the angel announces to the shepherds the good news of "great joy coming to the whole people" (Lk.2:10). This forms a fitting introduction to the Gloria, the great hymn sung by the choir of angels to celebrate the birth of the Saviour: "Glory to God in highest heaven, and on earth peace for men on whom his favour rests" (Lk.2:14). Yet, "the angel of the Lord upon the first Christmas Eve struck the key-note not only of the incarnation prelude but of the whole gospel".[3]

The Teaching of Jesus

The new joy brought into the world by Jesus finds expression in his teaching. In chapter six, we have Luke's version of the Beatitudes. In these, Jesus enunciates a new definition of "blessedness" or "happiness". The poor, the hungry, the sorrowful, and the persecuted are all pronounced "blessed" (*makarioi*—Lk.6:20-23). To them belongs "the kingdom of God" and they have "a rich reward in heaven". They can lay claim to the happy state usually reserved in ancient Greek literature for the gods and for specially privileged mortals; for man's true happiness does not lie in the amount of possessions (cf.Lk.12:15) but in the realisation of spiritual need and in the acceptance of God's gift in Jesus Christ. The person who does not find Christ a stumbling-block is truly happy (Lk.7:23). The felicity of such discipleship is superior to that of natural motherhood, even when the son is none other than the Messiah himself (Lk.11:27f.).

In the interpretation of the parable of the seed and the soils, there is a description of those whose acceptance of the gospel message is enthusiastic but superficial. They "receive the word with joy when they hear it, but have no root; they are believers for a while, but in the time of testing they desert" (Lk.8:13). A

better type of joy is that described in chapter ten of Luke's
Gospel. The seventy-two were jubilant over the subjection of
devils to them during their mission of evangelism (Lk.10:17;
cf.10:20), while Jesus rejoiced over the revelation given by God
to ordinary people (Lk.10:21). We have already discussed the
joy of Jesus in the previous chapter.

Festive joy occurs within the parable of the rich fool. The rich
man, having congratulated himself upon his good fortune,
thinks that he should "take life easy, eat, drink, and enjoy"
himself (Lk.12:19). Chapter thirteen has the statement of the
joy of the common people over the glorious things done by
Jesus (Lk.13:17). In chapter fourteen, the adjective "happy"
(*makarios*) is found twice in the course of the description of a
sabbath meal in the house of one of the Pharisees—once on the
lips of Jesus and once on those of a fellow-guest, whose pious
platitude concerning the happiness of the man who would sit at
the feast in the kingdom of God called forth from Jesus the
parable of the big dinner party (Lk.14:14f.).

This brings us to what has been called "that central gem of
the Gospel"[4]—chapter fifteen, which is the most joyful chapter
in the whole of the gospel of joy. Its nearest rival is the first
chapter, since each contains ten instances of words for joy. In
chapter fifteen, Luke relates three parables told by Jesus about
things that were lost and whose finding brought great joy to
their owners. When the shepherd had found the missing sheep,
he laid it on his shoulders rejoicing (Lk.15:5). Both he and the
housewife called neighbours and friends together to rejoice with
them over the recovery of the lost (Lk.15:6,9). Similarly, the
father gave a party in honour of his repentant son. When the
elder son objected to the festivities, he replied: "How could we
help celebrating this happy day?" (Lk.15:32) Four times over,
the same verb is used (*euphrainesthai*) in the sense of the festive
joy or merry-making that took place to celebrate the return of
the prodigal son (Lk.15:23,24,29,32).

All three parables were spoken to two sets of people who were
listening to Jesus' words. His audience comprised, firstly, the
tax-gatherers and other bad characters, who drew near wist-
fully; and, secondly, the Pharisees and the doctors of the law,
who were grumbling at the proximity of the former group. Jesus
told these parables as an apology for his interest in the depressed

classes of the Jewish community. He justified his attitude by saying, in effect, "This is how God thinks about these people and what God wants to do for them. They are 'lost' and must be found and brought back. I have come to call sinners to repentance." This point is driven home at the close of the first two parables. Jesus declared that just as the shepherd rejoiced over the recovery of the lost sheep and the housewife over the discovery of the lost coin, so there will be joy (*chara*) in heaven over one sinner who repents (Lk.15:7,10). This is the redemptive joy of Good—the joy that God has in forgiving the penitent. It was because of this joy of God in forgiveness that Jesus came into the world as Saviour of sinners.

The Joyful Reception of the Gospel

Chapter nineteen contains the stories of the joyful reception of Jesus into the house of Zacchaeus (Lk.19:6) and of the triumphal entry into Jerusalem on Palm Sunday to the accompaniment of the rejoicings and praises of the whole company of disciples (Lk.19:37). Such was the atmosphere of joy surrounding Jesus on this occasion that, when the Pharisees told him to silence his disciples, he replied that if they were quiet the very stones would shout aloud (Lk.19:40).

This joyful reception of the gospel finds a contrast in the joy of the enemies of Jesus. The chief priests "were greatly pleased" when Judas went to them with his offer to betray his Master (Lk.22:5). So, too, was Herod when Jesus was sent to him in chains by Pilate (Lk.23:8). The joy of the enemies of Jesus, however, was short-lived.

The joy of the disciples of Jesus is high-lighted in the final chapter of the Gospel. When the two Emmaus disciples had returned to Jerusalem to tell the eleven of their experience on the homeward road, the risen Christ appeared in the midst of his followers. So startled were they that they could not believe their eyes. "While they still disbelieved for joy and wondered" (Lk.24:41—RSV), Jesus asked for something to eat in order to prove his identity and his reality. Then, just as the Gospel opened with joy, so it closes on the same note. After leading his disciples out as far as Bethany and blessing them, Jesus parted from them. "And they returned to Jerusalem with great joy, and spent all their time in the temple praising God" (Lk.24:52f.).

This was the joy of men who were convinced of the exaltation of their risen Lord and who looked forward to the fulfilment of Christ's promise of the gift of the Holy Spirit (cf. Acts 1:4f.).

The Gospel of Joy

Such is the startling frequency of words for joy in St Luke's narrative. It is little wonder that it has been called "The Gospel of Joy". It is overflowing with gladness and good cheer. Its chief characters are always singing and praising God. It contains four great hymns that were to form the basis of the liturgy of the Christian church. The parables of Jesus recorded by Luke are full of joy and thanksgiving. Of the 53 instances of words for joy in Luke's Gospel, fourteen are in parables and another sixteen are in other sayings of our Lord.

Here, too, we find the joyful reception of the Word of God by the common people and by such a public figure as Zacchaeus, chief collector of taxes in Jericho. Running right through the narrative is that note of joy and of triumph—from the first chapters with their announcement of good news of great joy to the very last verses, when the disciples returned to the city of Jerusalem after witnessing the ascension of their risen Lord.

The Sequel to the Gospel of Joy

The same note of joy is visible in the Acts of the Apostles. We find it in Peter's sermon on the Day of Pentecost, where some verses from Psalm 16 are quoted as a prophecy of the resurrection of Jesus Christ. David is said to be speaking about Jesus: "I saw the Lord before me always ... so my heart was glad and my tongue exulted ... you will fill me with gladness with your presence" (Acts 2:25ff.—my own translation). The psalmist was carried beyond the confines of mere temporal existence. He felt assured that God would be able to deliver him even from the threat of corruption in Hades. Union with God, begun here and now, could not be dissolved by death, but would be continued into the next world, where he would enjoy the fellowship of God's presence. Thus did the psalmist grope his way towards a belief in a future life. As Christians, however, we can read with Peter a deeper and fuller meaning into the psalmist's words as we interpret them in the light of the resurrection and ascension of our Lord. Peter's sermon led to a great increase in the membership of the Christian church. All who believed shared their possessions, attended the temple daily, and, "breaking bread in private houses, shared their meals with unaffected joy" (Acts 2:46).

The growth of the church and the propagation of the new faith so annoyed the Jewish authorities that they arrested and cautioned Peter and John (Acts 4:3,18,23), the two apostles who were the ringleaders of the group of enthusiastic sectarians. When this did not succeed in checking the movement, the apostles were imprisoned (Acts 5:18). After they had been miraculously released from prison, they were brought before the Sanhedrin. On the advice of Gamaliel, the apostles were released after a flogging (Acts 5:40). Luke tells us that they "went out from the Council rejoicing that they had been found worthy to suffer indignity for the sake of the Name" (Acts 5:41).

After Stephen's reference to the false joy of the people of Israel over the golden calf made for them by Aaron in the absence of Moses (Acts 7:41), we read of the ever-widening circle of rejoicing that took place in connection with the spread of the Christian church throughout the Mediterranean world. Philip's preaching of Christ caused much joy in a city of Samaria (Acts 8:8) and enabled the Queen of Ethiopia's chancellor of the exchequer to go on his way rejoicing after being baptized (Acts 8:39). The success of the mission to the Gentiles in Antioch gladdened the heart of Barnabas (Acts 11:23).

Rhoda's joy at hearing Peter outside the door of the house where the prayer-meeting was being held (Acts 12:14) is followed in the next chapter by the joy of the Gentiles at Pisidian Antioch over Paul's declaration that the word of God was for them as well as for Jews (Acts 13:48). Even after Paul and Barnabas had been driven out of the district, "the converts were filled with joy and with the Holy Spirit" (Acts 13:52). At Lystra on the same missionary journey Paul, in his sermon of rebuke to the people for regarding himself and Barnabas as gods, held up as the most striking witness to the gracious providence of God the fact that he satisfies our hearts with food and good cheer in plenty (Acts 14:17—cf. Luke's characteristic emphasis upon festive joy, as in Luke 15:23ff.). After their return to their base in Antioch in Syria, the two apostles were sent up to Jerusalem to confer with the church leaders on the position of Gentiles in the Christian church. On the way thither, their reports of success in Asia Minor to the Christians in Samaria and Phoenicia filled them with great rejoicing (Acts 15:3). Then when the Christians at Antioch in Syria read the apostolic decree issued at the end of the conference at Jerusalem in A.D.49, "they all rejoiced at the encouragement it brought" (Acts 15:31). This decree opens with this same Greek verb "to rejoice" (*chairein*) used as a greeting (Acts 15:23). One commentator suggests that a sublime significance can be read into this everyday formula when it is used as here by the faithful.[5]

The exultant joy of the early church at Jerusalem (Acts 2:46), which we have already noted above, is matched by the scene in the house of the Philippian jailer after he had washed the wounds of Paul and Silas and had himself been baptized by them, along with his whole family. The same exultant mood as had prevailed at Jerusalem invaded his house at Philippi as he "rejoiced with his whole household in his new-found faith in God" (Acts 16:34).

The adjective "blessed" (*makarios*) occurs twice in Acts—first, when Paul quotes to the Ephesian elders the otherwise unknown beatitude of Jesus: "Happiness lies more in giving than in receiving" (Acts 20:35). The second occasion is when the Apostle rejoices in his good fortune at having to make his defence before King Agrippa: "I consider myself fortunate, King Agrippa, that it is before you that I am to make my defence today ..." (Acts 26:2).

The only other significant occurrences of words for joy in Acts are words of encouragement—Jesus' words of cheer to Paul in the Roman barracks at Jerusalem (Acts 23:11), the Apostle's courageous reassurances to the sailors in the storm off Malta (Acts 27:22,25,36), and Paul's own taking of courage on meeting with the Roman Christians at the Three Taverns (Acts 28:15). Even Paul could have his moods of despondency, but his confidence returned and he forgot all about the hardships of the journey from Jerusalem when he saw this evidence of the presence and the work of Christ in Rome.

Thus it is that right through the Book of Acts as well as through the Gospel according to St Luke we can trace the joy of the good tidings brought by Jesus Christ. The story of "how they brought the good news from Jerusalem to Rome"[6] is one that is full of gladness and exultation. The third gospel is indeed justly called "The Gospel of Joy". Yet scarcely less joyful is its noble sequel—the second volume of "The History of the Rise of Christianity" dedicated to Theophilus and written by the beloved physician and travelling companion of the Apostle Paul.

15

JOY IN MATTHEW AND MARK

In contrast to Luke's Gospel, not very much of joy is to be found in either Matthew or Mark. True it is that words for joy appear twenty-nine times in Matthew and seven times in Mark, but in the case of the former thirteen of these instances are of the adjective *makarios* (see Chapter Eight), nine of them within the context of the beatitudes of the Sermon on the Mount. Apart from this word, "exultant joy" (*agallian*) appears once in Matthew, "courage" (*tharsein*) three times, and "inward joy" twelve times (*chara* and *chairein* each six times). Mark's Gospel contains two examples of "courage" (*tharsein*), three of "inward joy" (*chara* once and *chairein* twice), and two of "pleasure" (in the form of the adverb *hēdeōs*).

Wise Men and Beatitudes

Parallel to the proclamation of good tidings of great joy to the shepherds in Luke, we find in Matthew's Gospel the story of the wise men who came from the east. "At the sight of the star they were overjoyed" (Mt.2:10). They knew that they had reached their journey's end. Their mood is captured in the words of the hymn by W.C. Dix:

As with gladness men of old
Did the guiding star behold,
As with joy they hailed its light,
Leading onward, beaming bright,—
So, most gracious Lord, may we
Evermore be led to Thee.

The note of joy is not struck again till the Sermon on the Mount, which opens with the beatitudes. "In eight matchless sentences, Christ claims as his own the poor in spirit, those who mourn for sin, the meek, those who yearn for righteousness, the merciful, the pure in heart, the pacific, and those who suffer for righteousness' sake. These are the qualities and virtues he singles out for the special approbation of heaven."[1]

The joy that shines through these ten verses is specially mentioned by Montefiore, who writes: "There is a glow and passion about the whole passage which are unique: there is a certain religious character and 'ethos' about it which are marked and distinctive."[2] The beatitudes are rounded off with reference to the stern joy that should mark out Christians in time of persecution—a joy which looks forward to reward in heaven (Mt.5:12).

Take Heart!

In chapter 9, Matthew has two instances of the imperative of *tharsein* (see Chapter Five) on the lips of Jesus. The paralytic is told to "take heart" on account of the forgiveness of his sins (Mt.9:2). This was the result of the faith of his four friends who had brought him to Jesus. In the case of the woman with haemorrhage, it was her own personal faith that led to her recovery of health (Mt.9:22). Both these incidents are recorded also in Mark and in Luke, but neither of them makes use of the verb *tharsein*.

Mark uses this verb in his account of the healing of blind Bartimaeus at Jericho (Mk.10:49). Matthew follows Mark in using it in the incident on the Lake of Galilee after the feeding of the five thousand, when Jesus came to his disciples "walking on the lake" and dispelled their fears with his cry of reassurance (Mt.14:27 = Mk.6:50).

Joy in Parables of Jesus

The glad reception of the word of God appears in the parable of the sower and the soils. The rocky ground is a symbol for the man who hears the gospel message and is captured by it, but whose enthusiasm is short-lived (Mt.13:20 = Mk.4:16). More commendable is the inward joy (*chara*) of the man who found treasure hidden in a field. To such a person, the kingdom of heaven is so valuable that he is willing to sacrifice everything for its sake (Mt.13:44). The key-words in this parable are "for sheer joy". "When that great joy, surpassing all measure, seizes a man, it carries him away, penetrates his inmost being, sub-jugates his mind. All else seems valueless compared with that surpassing worth. No price is too great to pay."[3] A variant version of this parable is to be found in the Coptic Gospel of Thomas (GTh.109), but there the note of joy is expressed in a different way. The man who bought the field from its previous owners and who discovered the treasure while he was ploughing "began to lend money to whomever he wished".[4]

The parable of the lost sheep is "a parable of the redemptive joy of God".[5] Matthew tells us that the shepherd "is more delighted over that sheep than over the ninety-nine that never strayed" (Mt.18:13). Although Luke has preserved the original setting of this parable (Lk.15:3-7), it is Matthew who emphasizes God's joy in forgiveness. This is all the more true if, as Professor Jeremias argues, the concluding verse in Matthew's pericope should read: "There is joy in the heart of God when one of the very least is saved" (Mt.18:14). This verse would then agree with the first half of Luke 15:7.[6]

In the parable of the talents, the reward given to the two faithful servants is expressed in terms of joy (*chara*): "Come and share your master's delight" (Mt.25:21,23). It may well be that *chara* here means "a meal of joy".[7]

Easter Joy

The joy of Easter is seen in Matthew's account of the visit of "Mary of Magdala and the other Mary" to the garden tomb on the first day of the week. After the angel had spoken to them, "they hurried away from the tomb in awe and great joy, and ran to tell the disciples" (Mt.28:8). In Mark, on the other hand, "they said nothing to anybody, for they were afraid" (Mk.16:8). Both evangelists refer to the "awe" or "fear" (*phobos* in Mt. and the cognate verb *phobeisthai* in Mk.) felt by the women in face of the mystery of the empty tomb; but only in Matthew is it joined with "great joy". "This union of apparently opposite emotions is true to human nature. All powerful tides of gladness cause nervous thrills that feel like fear and trembling."[8]

Conclusion

Apart from two references in Mark to people who heard Jesus gladly (Mk.6:20; 12:37), the delight of the chief priests at Judas' offer of betrayal (Mk.14:11), four examples of the imperative of *chairein* used as a greeting (Mt.26:49; 27:29 = Mk.15:18; Mt.28:9), and four instances of *makarios* in beatitudes pronounced by Jesus (Mt.11:6; 13:16; 16:17; 24:46), the passages quoted above exhaust the occurrences of cognates and synonyms for joy in Matthew and Mark.

Nevertheless, there are other passages in which such words do not occur but which contain the note of joy that is inherent in Christianity. A question about fasting asked by the disciples of John the Baptist, for example, evoked from Jesus the comparison of his disciples to wedding guests (Mt.9:13 = Mk.2:19). Again, the sight of children playing at weddings and funerals in the marketplace suggested to Jesus a comparison between the festive joy of his own religion and the asceticism of that of John the Baptist (Mt.11:18ff.).

Or again, Jesus likened the kingdom of heaven to a marriage feast (Mt.22:2-14). "This parable is not fully understood," declares Professor Jeremias, "until attention is paid to the note of joy which rings through the summons: 'everything is ready'."[9]

Finally, the parable of the ten virgins begins on a note of joy (Mt.25:2). The kingdom of God is compared to the wedding, not to the ten girls. Jesus declared that the wedding-day has come and that the banquet is ready.[10]

In spite of all this, however, it remains true that Matthew and Mark fall far behind the third gospel in its quality of radiant joy and gladness. Written for other reasons than the Gentile Christian Gospel of Luke and from different points of view, they reflect personalities unlike that of the friend of the Apostle Paul. As a result, each of them bears its own peculiar characteristics, which make its contribution to the fund of knowledge regarding the earthly life and ministry of Jesus equally valuable with that of Luke even though the Christian conception of joy is not specially emphasized.

16

THE FULNESS OF JOY — JOHN

The Johannine literature makes its own peculiar contribution to the New Testament conception of joy even although cognates and synonyms for joy occur only thirty times—twenty-three times in the Fourth Gospel and seven times in the letters. "Exultant joy" (*agallian*) appears twice in the Gospel, "courage" (*tharsein*) once, and "blessedness" (*makarios*) twice. "Inward joy" (*chara/chairein*) is found a total of twenty-five times—eighteen in the Gospel and seven in the letters. Of the occurrences of *chairein*, however, three (Jn.19:3; 2 Jn.10f.) are in the sense of a greeting and do not require special notice in this chapter (see Chapter Ten).

Eschatological Tension

The uniqueness of the Johannine conception of Christian joy is due partly to the eschatological tension that is apparent, especially in the Fourth Gospel, between the "now" and the "not yet". Thus, for example, in his conversation with the woman of Samaria beside Jacob's well at Sychar, Jesus said: "The time approaches, indeed it is already here, when those who are real worshippers will worship the Father in spirit and in truth" (Jn.4:23). On the other hand, when a guest at the wedding in Cana, he said to his mother: "My hour has not yet come" (Jn.2:4). Throughout the Gospel, it is evident that the old Jewish eschatology has now been fulfilled in the coming of Jesus Christ. Yet a new Christian eschatology is put in its place. Both aspects can be seen with regard to joy in the Fourth Gospel.

The note of fulfilment is seen, first of all, in the joy of John the Baptist. He saw in the growing influence of Jesus the completion of his own mission. John used the wedding analogy found elsewhere on the lips of Jesus, but he extended it to include the friend of the bridegroom, to whom he likened himself. The duties of the friend were to arrange for and preside at the wedding and to stand before the bridal chamber until he heard the bridegroom's voice on his arrival. He "is overjoyed at hearing the bridegroom's voice". Likewise, the joy of the Baptist was fulfilled in the joy of Jesus (Jn.3:29).[1]

The prophet Amos (9:13) had sung of the wonderful days of the Messiah when the natural process of growth would be so speeded up that ploughman and reaper would work together. In the spiritual situation among the Samaritans after his conversation with the woman at Jacob's well, Jesus saw the signs of the promised age of fulfilment (Jn.4:36).

It is possible that the exultant, though fickle, joy of the Jews over John the Baptist (Jn.5:35) was due to the prospect of the imminent fulfilment of their messianic hopes that was held out by him in his preaching. There is evidence both in the New Testament and in Josephus that his work did provoke some messianic excitement.[2] The joy of Abraham (Jn.8:56)—if it refers to his present experience in heaven and not to the Jewish tradition of a vision[3]—would also be a reference to messianic fulfilment. The meaning may well be that Abraham in the other world was joyfully conscious of Christ's appearance in this world. This thought is taken up in the legends of the *descensus ad inferos*, where it is said that the news of Christ's arrival on earth caused joy among the Old Testament saints in Hades.[4]

In contrast to these passages containing "realized eschatology", there are references in the Fourth Gospel to joy that had yet to be fulfilled. Jesus foretold that the disciples would have cause to "weep and mourn", but that their sorrow would turn to joy when they saw him again after his resurrection (Jn. 16:20-22). "They may learn from the example of the mother how the bliss that awaits them will wipe out all memory of suffering."[5] The fulfilment of the promise is described in chapter 20, where we read that, "when the disciples saw the Lord, they were filled with joy" (Jn.20:20). Nevertheless, Jesus suggested to the disciples that their love for him ought to have made them rejoice even in anticipation. His departure would lead to his exaltation (Jn.14:28). In these various passages, the noun *chara* is used three times, and the cognate verb *chairein* four times.

The single occurrence of the verb *tharsein* in the Fourth Gospel also belongs to the time when Jesus was predicting sorrow and tribulation for his disciples in the world. In spite of everything, they will be able to rejoice because of Christ's victory over the world and over death (Jn.16:33). "It is not only that joy will take the place of sorrow, but the sorrow itself becomes joy ... The Christian joy and hope do not arise from an ignoring of the evil in the world, but from facing it at its worst."[6]

Fulness of Joy

Similar to this eschatological joy that has yet to be fulfilled is another Johannine characteristic—the use of the verb *plēroun* (= to make full, to fulfil) along with the words *chara* and *chairein*.[7] We have already noted the saying of John the Baptist in which he compared himself to the friend of the bridegroom whose joy has been fulfilled with the coming of the divine bridegroom (Jn.3:29). Jesus himself used this type of phrase in the course of the farewell discourses in the Fourth Gospel. We have studied two of these passages in connection with the joy of Jesus (see Chapter Thirteen), but they call for at least passing reference in this chapter also.

The teaching of Jesus to his disciples was given in order that they might share in the joy of unbroken fellowship with the Father and with himself as a result of obedience to his commandments (Jn.15:11). The purpose of the ascension and the exaltation was the promotion of the disciples to this "fulness of joy"—a joy that could be fulfilled only in the spiritual relationship with Christ that was to follow his resurrection (Jn.17:13). Finally, Jesus told his disciples that as a result of his presence with the Father a new economy of prayer was to be established—prayer in the name of Jesus. "The name of Christ is both the passport by which the disciples may claim access into the audience chamber of God, and the medium through which the Divine answer comes."[8] "So far you have asked nothing in my name. Ask and you will receive, that your joy may be complete" (Jn.16:24).

Fulness of joy, therefore, comes about only as a result of obedience to the commandments of Christ and of the divine fellowship that arises out of such obedience. On the basis of this communion with God, the disciples of Christ can expect an answer to prayers offered in the name of their Master, that is, prayers that are in accordance with his will. Nevertheless, since the joy of unbroken fellowship with the Father and with the Son can be realized in its perfection only in the next world, there remains implicit in the Johannine doctrine of joy the note of unfulfilled eschatology. This eschatological joy, however, can be experienced in anticipation even while we are in this world in so far as we obey the commands of Christ and receive an answer to our prayers in his name. Such fulness of joy must always be one of the characteristics of the Christian church when it is true to its vocation.

Johannine Letters

The teaching of the Fourth Gospel finds echoes in the Johannine letters. 1 John, for example, emphasizes the fact that part of the essential purpose of the church is to share with others the word of life. This letter was written in order to bring other people into the divine fellowship with the Father and with the Son—a fellowship that brought with it "fulness of joy" (1 Jn.1:4). "Herein lies the incentive to Christian witness. Those who have been entrusted with the word of life must share it with others. ... To preserve that fellowship as a selfishly treasured monopoly is to lose the fulness of joy."[9] Similarly, in 2 John, the author speaks of his proposed visit to "the lady chosen by God and her children" (2 Jn.1), the object being the same as that in view in writing 1 John—"that our joy may be complete" (2 Jn.12).

The joy of John the Elder is partly fulfilled by his reception of the news that some of the members of the church to which he writes the second letter are leading a truly Christian life. He expresses his pleasure in accordance with ancient epistolary practice near the beginning of his letter (2 Jn.4). The recipient of the third letter has also made John happy by following the teaching and example of Christ (3 Jn.3). In fact, nothing gave John greater joy than to hear that his converts remained true to the faith (3 Jn.4). Thus, according to the Johannine conception of Christianity, "fulness of joy" can come about only when the divine fellowship enjoyed by the Christian has inspired him to reach out in an effort to influence the lives of other people and when he has brought them also into the joyful experience of unbroken fellowship with God through Jesus Christ.

Benediction of Ministry and of Faith

Three remaining instances of words for joy in the Fourth Gospel—two of *makarios* and one of *chairein*—are of special interest since they highlight joy in Christian faith and in Christian service.

The joy of obedient service is found in Christ's benediction of ministry (Jn.13:17). Jesus had just given his disciples an example of true humility and of lowly service in stooping to wash their feet in the upper room. He told them that in like manner they should joyfully seek to serve each other in obedience to his will.

Joy in Christian faith is found in Christ's benediction of faith (Jn.20:29). Future disciples would be unable to come to faith in Christ by the path of sight. That way had been open to Jesus' first followers, who saw him in flesh as a human being and witnessed his miracles.

Jesus fully appreciated the evidential character of his miracles in spite of the fact that he refused to perform mighty acts to order for the purpose of convincing his sceptical opponents. When he heard of the death of Lazarus, he expressed his joy at his absence from Bethany at that time (Jn.11:15). "Although his friend had died and the sisters are in grief, Jesus rejoices because of his confidence not only that Lazarus will be called back to life, but because this sign of power will increase the faith of his disciples, and promote the glory of God."[10]

Summary of Joy in John

We can sum up and characterize the Johannine contribution to the New Testament conception of joy by picking out the phrase "the fulness of joy", provided we keep in mind also the eschatological tension that is apparent especially in the Fourth Gospel. Fulness of joy is possible here and now, as John the Baptist was the first to realize, on account of the coming of Christ to this world and more especially as a result of his resurrection, ascension and exaltation. During his earthly life, he himself enjoyed unbroken fellowship with the Father. He promised similar joy to all his followers—even to those future disciples who would have to rely entirely upon faith apart from sight—if they fulfilled the essential condition, namely, obedience to his commandments.

While this joy could be experienced to a certain extent by the disciples during the earthly ministry of Jesus, its fulfilment could only come with the establishment of the new spiritual relationship that was to succeed his exaltation. In the end, however, it has to be said that the full and perfect realization of unbroken fellowship with God can only come outwith this world of time and space, even although it may be anticipated in part here and now. This is the logical conclusion of the Johannine argument with regard to "fulness of joy", though it never comes explicitly to the surface either in the Fourth Gospel or in the Johannine Letters.

17

JOY IN THE LORD — PAUL

Of all the New Testament writers, the Apostle Paul has the most references to joy in its various aspects. This should not surprise us, for his extant correspondence comprises ten of the twenty-seven canonical books.[1] These Pauline letters contain 132 of the 326 instances of our cognates and synonyms, that is, 40%. There are also five examples in the Pastoral Letters, which many scholars believe were not written entirely by Paul even though they may contain genuine fragments of several letters written by him.[2] Each of these thirteen letters—the Paulines and the Pastorals—has at least one of these words for joy, while a few have several. The four largest contributors to the total are the letter to the Romans (with 24), 1 and 2 Corinthians (with 17 and 53 respectively), and Philippians (with 19). Three of the groups of words for joy are missing—"exultant joy" (*agallian*), "optimism" (*euthumein*) and "leaping for joy" (*skirtan*); but all the other groups are represented, as we can see from the accompanying table.

From first to last, Christianity for Paul was a religion not only of grace but also of joy.[3] Since his letters are the earliest books of the New Testament, he was the first person to give literary expression to this conception. Some twenty years before Luke wrote his gospel of joy, the Apostle Paul had dictated his

	Gladness (euphrainein/ euphrosunē)	Pleasure (hēdonē/hēdus/ hēdeōs)	Courage (tharsein/ tharrein/tharsos)	Hilarity (hilaros/hilarotēs)	Boasting (kauchasthai/ kauchēma/kauchēsis)	Blessedness (makarios/ makarizein/makarismos)	Inward Joy (chairein/chara)	Shared Joy (sunchairein)	
Gal.	1	-	-	-	3	1	1	-	6
1 Thess.	-	-	-	-	1	-	6	-	7
2 Thess.	-	-	-	-	1	-	-	-	1
1 Cor.	-	-	-	-	10	1	4	2	17
2 Cor.	1	3	5	1	29	-	14	-	53
Rom.	1	-	-	1	10	5	7	-	24
Col.	-	-	-	-	-	-	3	-	3
Phmn.	-	-	-	-	-	-	1	-	1
Ephes.	-	-	-	-	1	-	-	-	1
Phil.	-	-	-	-	3	-	14	2	19
Pastorals	-	1	-	-	-	3	1	-	5

letters to various churches and individuals and in so doing had preserved for posterity his convictions concerning the basic truths of Christianity. For these reasons—the abundance of the vocabulary of joy in his writings and their early date—it is important to try and discover the mind of Paul. What did he think about the Christian conception of joy? How did he use these cognates and synonyms?

We shall study Paul's letters in what I consider to be their chronological order—though there is no unanimity among scholars on this matter.

Joyful Freedom (Galatians)

The letter to the Galatians may have been written about A.D. 48 or 49—shortly after Paul's first missionary journey recorded in the Acts of the Apostles and before his visit to Jerusalem for the Apostolic Council (Acts 15). At this council, the question of the free admittance of Gentiles into the Christian Church was settled once and for all time.

Since the Apostle's departure from the district of Galatia, Judaizers have been at work trying to stir up trouble in the churches founded by Paul.[4] To counteract their influence, Paul reminds the Galatians of the pleasure with which they had received him (Gal.4:15). In contrast to his opponents, he boldly declares his reliance solely upon the cross and all it stood for. "God forbid that I should boast of anything but the cross of our Lord Jesus Christ" (Gal.6:14). Just before this great assertion, however, Paul seems to contradict his resolve to "boast joyfully" (*kauchasthai*) only in the cross by saying that each one should "test his own work, and then his reason to boast will be in himself alone and not in his neighbour" (Gal.6:4—RSV). The truth is that the Apostle really knows two legitimate objects of boasting, although both lead back to the grace of God in Christ. Every believer ought to be able to glory not only in the cross of the Lord Jesus Christ seen as the outreaching of the love of God to mankind, but also in the work accomplished by himself in fulfilling the law of Christ (Gal.6:2) by showing the divine love to others. The Christian's joyful boasting is both in the cross of his Lord and in his own faithful service undertaken as a result of Christ's sacrificial death. Yet the two grounds of glorying can be seen as essentially one—the

love of God revealed *par excellence* in the cross of Christ and
going out to men through Christian witness and service. This
divine love (*agapē*) transcends all human, man-made
institutions such as circumcision; for with the coming of Jesus
Christ law has been superseded by grace, which is freely
bestowed by God upon men unworthy though they are.

In his controversy with those Judaizers who wish to be under
the law instead of under grace, Paul uses an allegory—referring
to the story of Abraham's two sons, one by a slave and the other
by his free wife. To the former, he likens those who remain in
slavery to the Jewish Law, while to the latter he compares the
Christian church. The founding of the church had been delayed,
as had been the birth of Isaac. Now, like Sarah, the church can
rejoice over the grace of God (Gal.4:27).

Finally, it is in this letter that Paul enumerates nine products
of the Spirit that together form the unity of a truly Christian
character (Gal.5:22f.). Love comes first since without it all
other gifts and virtues are worthless (cf. 1 Cor.13:1-3,13). The
fact that joy (*chara*) comes second in the list shows the
prominent place that it had in the thought of the Apostle Paul
with regard to the Christian personality. While Christian
freedom is the main theme of this letter, such freedom must be
characterized by a joyful attitude to life; for joy is one of the
essential characteristics of those who live by the Spirit.
Christians should be able to rejoice in their new-found freedom
no matter what the circumstances are.

Mutual Joy (1 and 2 Thessalonians)

In these two letters, there are eight instances of words for joy.
"Inward joy" occurs six times (*chara* four times and *chairein*
twice), while "boasting" appears twice (*kauchēsis* in 1 Thessalonians and *enkauchasthai* in 2 Thessalonians).

The church at Thessalonica was one in which the Apostle
appears to have taken particular delight. It had been founded by
him round about the year A.D. 50 in the course of his second
missionary journey. It had grown from strength to strength in
spite of a certain amount of opposition and persecution. Those
who had been influenced by Paul's preaching had undergone
grave suffering as a result. Yet they "rejoiced in the Holy
Spirit" and had become an example to the Christians in the

surrounding districts (1 Thess.1:6f.). "Their joyful example
under persecution had communicated itself to others over a
wide area."[5] Their joy, like that of Jesus himself, was the result
of divine inspiration. The Holy Spirit had been at work not only
in the missionaries who had visited the city, but also in the
people who had heard them. "The same Spirit which gave
strength and assurance to the preachers wrought in the converts
a joyful acceptance of the message which was not checked by
the violent opposition of the synagogue aided by a truculent
mob."[6]

Paul's pride in the Thessalonian Christians is clearly shown
when he asks two rhetorical questions and supplies the answer
to them himself: "What hope or joy (*chara*) or crown of pride
(*kauchēsis*) is there for us, what indeed but you, when we stand
before our Lord Jesus Christ at his coming? It is you indeed
who are our glory and joy" (1 Thess.2:19f.).[7] The Apostle
supplies further evidence of his affection for his readers in the
following chapter when he asks another question: "What
thanks can we return to God for you? What thanks for all the
joy you have brought us, making us rejoice before our God ..."
(1 Thess.3:9).

We thus see in 1 Thessalonians the mutual joy between Paul
and his converts at Thessalonica. They had welcomed him to
their city with joy and had received the gospel as a result of his
preaching. Their Christian loyalty and witness encouraged other
churches in Greece and cheered the heart of the Apostle. He felt
that he could look upon them as part of the crown of victory
that would be his at the coming of the Lord Jesus Christ. Before
he closed the letter, he exhorted them once again to the attitude
of joy as being part of "the standing orders of the gospel"[8]:
"Be always joyful; pray continually; give thanks to God
whatever happens; for this is what God in Christ wills for you"
(1 Thess.5:16f.). No matter what their circumstances are,
Christians are expected to be men and women of joy, prayer,
and thanksgiving. Such is God's will for them. "We must
always have the music of the gospel in our hearts in its own
proper key."[9]

The same note of joyful thanksgiving over the Thessalonian
Christians is struck again at the beginning of 2 Thessalonians by
means of the compound verb *enkauchasthai* (used only here in

the New Testament). Paul declares that the growth of faith and love amongst his readers makes them the object of joyful boasting on his part amongst the congregations of God's people (2 Thess.1:4).

Right and Wrong Boasting (1 and 2 Corinthians)

It is in the letters to the Corinthians that more than 50% of the Pauline instances of our vocabulary for joy occurs—70 out of the total of 132—17 in 1 Corinthians and 53 in 2 Corinthians. Of these 70 examples, 39 are of the verb *kauchasthai* (= to boast) and its cognates.

Paul's contacts with Corinth began about the year A.D.50 during his second missionary journey. He stayed in the city on that occasion for some eighteen months. His work was done for the most part amongst the poorer and less privileged members of the community since it was to them that the gospel had most appeal. Yet through all his success the Apostle saw the purpose of God. "To shame the wise, God has chosen what the world counts folly. ... And so there is no place for human pride in the presence of God" (1 Cor.1:26-29). He summed up the matter by reminding his readers of their true and only ground for boasting: "And so (in the words of Scripture), 'If a man must boast, let him boast of the Lord' " (1 Cor.1:31)—an echo of words written by the prophet Jeremiah.

By the time Paul wrote the letter we know as 1 Corinthians, the brilliant Alexandrian teacher Apollos had arrived and had led many Jews into the faith through his preaching. Jealous comparisons between him and Paul had arisen among their respective adherents and party-strife was rampant in the Church. Paul rebuked them (1 Cor.3:21) and reminded them that there was only one head of the church—Christ himself (1 Cor.3:23). He then declared that to run wild after one teacher to the disparagement of another was to give way to spiritual pride, since all that they had had been given to them (1 Cor.4:7).

From this ecclesiastical question, Paul turns to the problem of discipline in connection with a scandalous case of immorality which the church at Corinth had condoned. Having attacked the spiritual pride lying behind such moral laxity (1 Cor.5:6), Paul proceeds to point out that since "the sacrifice is offered—Christ himself", we ought to do away with all corruption and wickedness and live true and sincere Christian lives in a continual festival of joy (1 Cor.5:7f.). The Greek word used here is *heortazein* (= to keep festival), and it is found only here in the New Testament. The festival spoken of is not the Jewish Passover nor even the Christian Eucharist. The reference is to the whole Christian life that is lived in perfect freedom from all anxious worries and fears. Paul realized that one essential condition for Christian joy was ethical purity, the supreme motive for which lay in the sacrifice of Jesus Christ for sins. Thus relying upon Christ's finished work of reconciliation and redemption, the Christian ought to aim at purity and sincerity and to make his whole life a festal celebration.

In chapter 7, where Paul gives advice on Christian marriage, he declares that all earthly things and pleasures have to be enjoyed as means and not ends since this world is all a fleeting show. From now on, those who rejoice must live as though they were not rejoicing (1 Cor.7:30), just as those who mourn are counselled to live as though they were not mourning. The Apostle proceeds to give his judgment on the remarriage of widows in the light of what he felt to be the imminent return of Christ. He does not regard celibacy as a holier state than matrimony, but considers that it gives greater freedom for Christian service. Thus he feels that a widow "is better off (*makarios*) as she is" (1 Cor.7:40).

Although Paul himself could have looked to the churches he had founded for financial support as an apostle, he nevertheless worked with his hands that the gospel might thereby be furthered. He looked upon this as a legitimate ground for boasting since it was for the promotion of Christ's kingdom (1 Cor.9:15). He felt that preaching itself gave him no such ground, since necessity was laid upon him to preach the gospel. He looked for no other reward than that contained in the satisfaction of offering the gospel to everyone. At first sight, such boasting seems to run counter to Paul's general position of refusing to glory except in Christ. Yet Paul's sole object was the greater freedom he thereby gained for the service of Christ and his gospel. His boasting here, as always, is still "in the Lord".

One of the difficulties that had cropped up in the Corinthian church was due to the pride of certain members over particular spiritual gifts, such as speaking with tongues. Paul insists that

all the activities of the Christian community—even the less
spectacular ones—are the result of the working of the Holy
Spirit. Such unity of the Spirit corresponds to the unity of
various parts of the human body. "If one organ suffers, they all
suffer together. If one flourishes, they all rejoice together" (1
Cor.12:26). Such unity should be seen within the church, which
is the body of Christ. Spiritual gifts are worthless apart from
love (*agapē*)—even martyrdom does not have any value on its
own (1 Cor.13:3). One of the characteristics of love is that it
"does not gloat over other men's sins, but delights in the truth"
(1 Cor.13:6).

In chapter 15, Paul comes to the most important subject of
all—the resurrection of the body. This is connected with the
question as to whether or not Christ really rose from the dead.
Paul declares that he has staked his whole life and ministry upon
belief in the resurrection of Jesus Christ. For this conviction, he
suffers mortal danger every day. The truth of this statement is
backed up by an oath concerning his feelings of pride for the
Corinthian Church (1 Cor.15:31).

Finally, after giving some items of news and certain
commissions, Paul thanks the Corinthians for the joy that he
has had in welcoming their three messengers—Stephanas,
Fortunatus and Achaicus. He had rejoiced at their coming since
they had made up for the absence of his readers by giving the
Apostle news of them (1 Cor.16:17f.).

Second Corinthians

Between the writing of 1 and 2 Corinthians, Paul paid them
"a painful visit" (2 Cor.2:1) and wrote them a severe letter (see
2 Cor.2:4). His strained relations can be inferred from parts of 2
Corinthians; for example, from the beginning of chapter two,
where three instances of our vocabulary occur within two verses
(2 Cor.2:2f.).

By the time the letter we know as 2 Corinthians was written,
reconciliation had taken place and the mutual joy of the Apostle
and his converts had been restored. With a clear conscience,
Paul can boast of his good behaviour both in the world at large
and toward them in particular (2 Cor.1:12). He trusts that they
will realize the full extent of their legitimate pride in him (2
Cor.1:14). The word used in this verse is *kauchēma* (= the thing

boasted of) in contrast to *kauchēsis* (= the act of boasting—see verse 12). Paul can be "a ground of boasting" for his converts at Corinth in their controversy with his opponents. His aim in writing this letter is not to commend himself to them again but rather to uphold them in their joyful pride (2 Cor.5:12). It was because of all this that the Apostle had desired to visit Corinth on his way to Macedonia as well as on his return journey. He wanted to give them the joy of a double visit (2 Cor.1:15). Through it all, Paul insists that he does not wish to give the impression of lording it over their faith. He maintains that his work was undertaken for the promotion of their joy (2 Cor.1:24).

Just as Paul's Corinthian readers can be proud of him, so he also can glory in them once again as a result of the healing of the threatened breach with them and the restoration of his great confidence in them (2 Cor.7:16). He is overjoyed on their account in spite of his afflictions (2 Cor.7:4). His joy was caused by the news brought to him by Titus of their continued loyalty to himself and of their repentance (2 Cor.7:7,9). Paul could rejoice even more because of the joy felt by Titus over the good news he had brought to the Apostle—news which had served to substantiate the pride in the Corinthians that Paul had previously expressed in his presence (2 Cor.7:13f.).

In chapters three to six, there almost appears to be an interruption in the main argument of the letter. Paul turns aside from his *apologia pro sua vita* and from boasting in order to give his reflections on the apostolic office and on the Christian hope. He declares, amongst other things, that whatever happens to him he can always be of good courage on account of his hope of going "to live with the Lord" (2 Cor.5:8). In the following chapter, he puts forward his apostolic credentials and emphasizes the fact that he can still rejoice in spite of everything (2 Cor.6:10).

When we turn to chapter eight, we find that Paul has had an axe to grind. He is anxious about the collection he is making for the church at Jerusalem. The Macedonian Christians are held up as an example in generous giving. "They have been so exuberantly happy that ... they have shown themselves lavishly open-handed" (2 Cor.8:2). The Corinthians are urged to follow suit since the Apostle has been boasting to other churches about their readiness to help (2 Cor.8:24; 9:2). For this purpose, he is sending messengers to them shortly to collect their offerings "to ensure that what we have said about you should not prove to be an empty boast" (2 Cor.9:3). To round off his appeal, Paul declares that "God loves a cheerful (*hilaros*) giver" and points to the example set by God, who himself is generous in supplying all our needs and has crowned his blessings to us by "his gift beyond words" (2 Cor.9:7-15).

There is such a complete change of tone and subject-matter at the beginning of the next chapter that some scholars have thought that in chapters ten to thirteen we have part of the severe letter (see 2 Cor.2:4). A preferable theory is that the Apostle now turns to deal with the still hostile element in the Corinthian church. Up to this point, he has been describing his thankful confidence in the Corinthians, most of whom are faithful to him; but he remembers the recalcitrant minority and upbraids them now in ironical fashion. His detractors have been saying that he is "so feeble when I am face to face with you, so brave (*tharrein*) when I am away" (2 Cor.10:1). Paul begs his readers, or at least some of them, to mend their ways so that he will not have to show "such bravery when I come, for I reckon I could put on as bold a face as you please against those who charge us with moral weakness" (2 Cor.10:2). He implores them not to force him to use his apostolic authority even though he does boast of it somewhat too much (2 Cor.10:8).

Paul has his opponents in mind again when he declares that he will not boast beyond limit in other men's labours. As the faith of the Corinthian Christians is strengthened he hopes to extend his preaching mission elsewhere, "never priding ourselves on work already done in another man's sphere" (2 Cor. 10:13-16). This is precisely what others have been doing with regard to his own work in Corinth. They have been trying to win Paul's converts away from their loyalty to him and to the gospel as he had preached it to them. In this connection, Paul recalls again the quotation he has already used from Jeremiah: "If a man must boast, let him boast of the Lord" (2 Cor.10:17).

The fact that Paul had refused to take any salary from the Corinthian church had provided his enemies with a ready-made weapon in their attack upon him. They called in question his apostolic authority since, of his own free will, he did not accept what was his due as an apostle. Paul now declares his resolve to maintain his financial independence (2 Cor.11:10-12). In spite of his efforts to refrain from boasting, Paul feels that he is driven to it by his opponents at Corinth. He prefaces his remarks on self-glorying by assuming the mask of a fool in so doing (2 Cor.11:16). Nevertheless, he is careful to repudiate divine inspiration for such glorying in worldly things (2 Cor.11:17), knowing that his readers will bear with him in his foolishness since they themselves are wise (2 Cor.11:19). In this ironical fashion, he tries to excuse himself for listing his sufferings as an apostle of Jesus Christ and for appearing to glory in them. Then he declares that, if he must boast—even though nothing is to be gained by it, he will boast in his own weaknesses so that the power of Christ may rest upon him (2 Cor.11:30; 12:1,5,6,9), and that the faith of the Corinthians may thereby be strengthened. He can rejoice in his own sufferings provided that they are strong in faith (2 Cor.13:9; cf.12:15). For the sake of their souls, he will gladly spend himself to the limit (2 Cor.12:15).

At the end of chapter thirteen, the Apostle concludes his message to the Corinthians in several short, abrupt sentences. The first of these contains the verb *chairein* without any strong signification of joy but rather as a closing greeting: "And now, my friends, farewell" (2 Cor.13:11).

Paul's Theology of Joy Summarized

It is in the letter to the Romans that we find the fullest expression of Paul's gospel. It is here that we have the most systematic presentation of his theological position. As a result, it is natural for us to expect to find in this letter a summary of Paul's views on the place of joy in the Christian religion. Our expectation is not disappointed.

To begin with, we find here a summary of Paul's views on boasting. Twelve of the twenty-four instances of words for joy contained in this letter are concerned with this aspect of the matter. Paul insists that no man can boast before God, neither Jew nor Gentile. The Jew who relies upon the Law and boasts of his relation to God dishonours God by breaking the Law (Rom.2:17,23). Even if it were possible to keep the Law in its entirety, any boasting in one's achievements would be ruled out of the count. Justification is possible only through faith, quite apart from any consideration of works (Rom.3:27). Paul proceeds to anticipate any possible Jewish appeal to the case of Abraham as an example of justification by works. "If Abraham was justified by anything he had done, then he has a ground for pride (*kauchēma*). But he has no such ground before God" (Rom.4:2). Then he backs up his general position by using as an Old Testament proof-text the opening verse of Psalm 32, where "David speaks of the happiness (*makarismos*) of the man whom God 'counts' as just, apart from any specific acts of justice" (Rom.4:6). The psalmist had sung of the blessedness of the man who has experienced the forgiveness of his sins and against whom the Lord does not count his sins. Paul asks whether this blessing was confined to the circumcised. He argues that the circumcision of the patriarch was only a sign or a seal of the acceptance with God that he had enjoyed while he was as uncircumcised as any Gentile (Rom.4:7ff.).

So much for the boasting of the Jews. In chapter eleven, Paul warns Gentiles not to exult over the rejection of Israel. Every spiritual blessing they enjoy comes to them on account of their connection with that nation. If they are like a wild olive shoot that has been grafted in to take the place of despised branches that have been broken off, they must not exult over (*kata-kauchasthai*) those branches since "it is not you who sustain the root: the root sustains you" (Rom.11:17f.).

Nevertheless, Paul did not preclude the idea of boasting altogether. Christians can boast in their hope of sharing the glory of God. Such elation of spirit is not dampened by any sufferings they have to endure in the present world. Being at peace with God, they no longer feel that things are against them. On the contrary, outward circumstances can be joyfully accepted as factors in their moral and spiritual progress (Rom.5:2ff.). "But that is not all: we also exult (*kauchasthai*) in God through our Lord Jesus, through whom we have been granted reconciliation" (Rom.5:11). Such joyful boasting is possible for all Christians; but the Apostle himself has further ground for glorying, namely, in the work that he has accomplished for Christ among Gentiles (Rom.15:17).

In the ethical section of Romans (Rom.12:1—15:13), several aspects of joy are brought to our attention. One of these is the idea of joy in hope—an idea we have already seen in chapter five. It is repeated in chapter twelve with the verb *chairein*: "Let hope keep you joyful." The idea of suffering is also prominent, as in chapter five, since this command is followed by another: "In trouble stand firm" (Rom.12:12). In addition, chapter twelve contains some advice on "pastoral duties", though the words are addressed to all Christians and not merely to the leaders of the church. Those who "give to charity" are to do so "with all the heart" (Rom.12:8—*hilarotēs*), while sympathy is recommended generally: "With the joyful be joyful (*chairein*), and mourn with the mourners" (Rom.12:15). The ability to adapt himself to the circumstances of those he wishes to help is indispensable to the Christian, as also is the quality of cheerfulness.

"Inward joy" (*chara*) occurs twice in these chapters in close association with the Holy Spirit. Since Paul considered that the joy of the Christian was inspired by God, he could speak of "joy in the Holy Spirit", but other qualities such as righteousness and peace were also regarded by him as being due to the action of God in human life. He believed that when a man allowed himself to be controlled by God's will these various characteristics emerged in his life (Rom.14:17). Joy and peace are again united with the power of the Holy Spirit in the prayer with which the Apostle rounds off this ethical section of his letter, but two other great keynotes of the Christian life are also linked with them—faith and hope (Rom.15:13). The joy and peace that God imparts to the Christian both rest on faith, while faith itself, with hope, its companion, can come about only through the gracious indwelling of God in the human heart through the Holy Spirit. Thus the whole life of the Christian believer—his faith, hope, and love, and the joy and peace that flow from the assurance of faith—is divinely inspired.

The value of having a clear conscience with regard to one's actions is upheld by Paul in his dealing with the question of scruples concerning food. Irrational prejudices and superstitious taboos cause needless fears and worries. "Happy (*makarios*) is the man who can make his decision with a clear conscience" (Rom.14:22).

Just before he closes this ethical section of the letter, the Apostle puts in a final word for mutual tolerance and cooperation between various groups within the Christian church —between weak and strong, between Jews and Gentiles. In connection with the overstepping of racial barriers, he can quote several Old Testament texts, including one from Deuteronomy: "As Scripture says, ... 'Gentiles, make merry (*euphrainesthai*) with his own people' " (Rom.15:10; Deut.32:43).

The letter to the Romans is almost finished—but before Tertius is allowed to lay down his pen, the Apostle adds some personal remarks. Amongst other items of news, he reminds the Roman Christians of his intention of visiting their city and he asks them to pray for the working out of his plans, "so that by his will I may come to you in a happy frame of mind (*chara*) and enjoy a time of rest with you" (Rom.15:32).

Thus, in the letter to the Romans, we find Paul dealing with almost every aspect of his contribution to the Christian conception of joy according to the New Testament. Having refuted any Jewish or Gentile claim to self-glory, he points to the only legitimate kind of exultation before God—joyful boasting in the Lord Jesus Christ and in the hope of sharing his glory. Such an eschatological element is present also in the ability to rejoice in the midst of sufferings, but Christian joy is by no means confined to the future. It can be experienced here and now as a result of our reconciliation with God through Jesus Christ and through the inspiration of the Holy Spirit. Joy, as a mood of faith, can therefore be the expression of the divine within him by the Christian in all his dealings with his neighbours and in his fellowship with other Christians.

Letters from Prison

Of the four prison letters, Colossians, Philemon and Ephesians stand apart from Philippians both in style and in subject-matter. If they were all written, as tradition holds, during Paul's imprisonment at Rome towards the end of his life, it may be that the first three were composed at the beginning of that period in A.D.60 or 61, while the letter to the Philippians may have been composed up to two years later. Our immediate concern, however, is not with critical questions of date. As far as the vocabulary of these letters is concerned, the first three have comparatively few words for joy—only five in all (three in Colossians, and one each in Philemon and Ephesians); while the letter to the Philippians has nineteen.

The main contribution of the letter to the Colossians to Paul's conception of joy is its insistence upon the possibility of such an attitude in the midst of sufferings and trials. In the introduction to the letter, after the usual salutation and thanksgiving, the Apostle utters a prayer that his readers may be strengthened "with ample power to meet whatever comes with fortitude, patience and joy (*chara*)" (Col.1:11). This "inward joy" should be accompanied by thanksgiving to God for the tremendous gifts of his grace to us in Jesus Christ—our share in "the heritage of God's people in the realm of light", our deliverance from "the domain of darkness", and our membership in "the kingdom of his dear Son, in whom our release is secured and our sins forgiven" (Col.1:12-14). All these blessings ought to make us joyful in spite of any trials that we are called upon to endure patiently. The inclusion of joy in the list of Christian virtues at this point is a necessary reminder since "the peculiar danger of the exercise of these qualities (viz. endurance and patience) is that it tends to produce a certain gloominess or sourness of disposition. The remedy is that the Christian should be so filled with joy that he is able to meet all his trials with a buoyant sense of mastery."[10]

Before the end of chapter one, Paul shows that he himself practises what he preaches in this regard, for he declares triumphantly: "It is now my happiness (*chairein*) to suffer for you" (Col.1:24). Since his imprisonment was the direct result of his work as an apostle, he could speak of it as being for the sake of Christians at Colossae and elsewhere. He could also rejoice in sharing the afflictions that Christ himself bore for his people. As a "servant by virtue of the task assigned to me by God for your benefit" (Col.1:25), Paul felt himself bound to rejoice in Christ's service, even when that service involved suffering. This joy was possible at the very moment of greatest trial. "It is easy to say fine things about patience in sufferings and triumph in sorrow when we are prosperous and comfortable; but it is different when we are in the furnace. This man, with the chain on his wrist, and the iron entering his soul, with his life in danger, and all the future uncertain, can say, '*Now* I rejoice.' This bird sings in a darkened cage."[11]

The third reference to joy in Colossians comes in the section of the letter in which the Apostle emphasizes his great concern for his readers. Even though he is absent from them in body, he is present with them in spirit, rejoicing (*chairein*) "to see your orderly array and the firm front which your faith in Christ presents" (Col.2:5). His joy over the Colossian church was occasioned by the fact that, in spite of heretical views that were being put forward by some, the majority were holding firm to the true apostolic doctrine. It was to encourage and uphold them in their loyalty to the faith that this letter was written.

The letter to Philemon, the most letter-like document in the New Testament, is closely associated with the letter to the Colossians. They were sent together by the hands of Tychicus to the city of Colossae. While the letter to the Colossians was sent to the church in general, the letter to Philemon was to be delivered to one particular member. Before the Apostle gets down to the main purpose of writing this letter, that is, to speak on behalf of the runaway slave Onesimus, he tells his correspondent of his delight (*chara*) at hearing good reports of his Christian life and witness (Phlm.7). Philemon seems to have been a leading member of the church at Colossae. He has put the Christians of the city in his debt by some recent act of love (*agapē*) as well as by allowing them to meet in his house for worship. His former good deeds make it easier for the Apostle to approach him on the delicate matter of his slave. Nevertheless, Paul feels that it requires all the tact he can muster to interfere in this domestic issue. He hopes to derive still more joy through a further demonstration of Philemon's love, this time toward Onesimus.

The verb *kauchasthai* (= to boast) occurs once in the letter to the Ephesians in the course of a passage on justification. Paul reminds his readers that it is by grace that they have been saved and not because of any merit on their own part. The reason for such depreciation of works by God is stated to be that "there is nothing for anyone to boast of" (Eph.2:9). This idea is characteristic of Paul, being especially prominent, as we have seen, in the letters to the Corinthians and to the Romans.

The Letter of Joy

The joy of Paul comes to its climax in the letter to the Philippians, whether or not this letter can be regarded as his "swan-song". No fewer than nineteen times do we find instances of words for joy here. "Inward joy" appears sixteen times (*chara* five times, *chairein* nine times and *sunchairein* twice), and "boasting" three times (*kauchēma* twice and *kauchasthai* once). Several aspects of the Christian conception of joy come before us in these various references.

After the opening salutation in the first two verses, there comes a joyful thanksgiving for the Christians at Philippi. Paul declares that he has no need to force himself to pray for his readers since their attitude towards him makes the task easy. "When I pray for you all, my prayers are always joyful (*chara*)" (Phil.1:4). This joy is more than the pleasure of friendship. The Apostle rejoices not only in the particular qualities of the church at Philippi. He is thankful that there are Christians in that city and for the part that they have played in the work of the gospel from the time of their conversion (Phil.1:5). Nevertheless, the Philippian Christians have given Paul special reason to be thankful for them in that they have recently revived their concern in him by sending a gift of money by the hand of Epaphroditus (Phil.4:10). Although they are thus already a source of great joy to the Apostle, being his "joy (*chara*) and crown" (Phil.4:1), his joy is not yet complete. There was a certain amount of disharmony in the church at Philippi. Paul urges his readers to "fill up my cup of happiness (*chara*) by thinking and feeling alike" (Phil.2:2).

In the course of chapter two, the Philippians are reminded of their duty as Christians to work out their own salvation "in fear and trembling" (Phil.2:12) and to "shine like stars in a dark world and proffer the word of life" (Phil.2:15). Paul argues that their success in these regards will be a cause of boasting (*kauchēma*) to him in the day of Christ inasmuch as they will prove that he had not run in vain nor laboured in vain (Phil.2:16). This will not be boastful self-glory. All that sort of thing is ruled out as far as the Christian is concerned. Rather will it be the legitimate joy of a servant of Jesus Christ over work accomplished for his Master. The mention of his labours for the Christians at Philippi leads the Apostle on to say that there is no sacrifice that he would not joyfully make on their behalf. Even if he should be poured out as a libation in addition to the sacrifice of faith that they are already offering to God, both he and they will have cause for joy since his sacrifice would be for the promotion of their salvation (Phil.2:17f.—*chairein* and *sunchairein* each occur twice in these two verses).

Another reason for joy in the mind of Paul appears in this letter. In spite of the fact that he is in prison, "Christ is set forth, and for that I rejoice (*chairein*)" (Phil.1:18). This he can do even although some of those who preach the gospel are doing so from envy and rivalry and in order to afflict him in his imprisonment. Paul might very well have written as Wesley did to some Irish friends: "I blame all even that speak the truth otherwise than in love. Keenness of spirit and tartness of language are never to be commended."[12] The Apostle's tone is conciliatory, however, and more after the style of an extract from the letters of Cobden: "To my humble apprehension, it is as unwise as it is unjust in any kind of political warfare to assail those who are disposed to co-operate, however slightly, in the attempt to overthrow a formidable and uncompromising enemy."[13] So it was to Paul in his fight against evil and anti-Christian forces. He is resolved to continue to rejoice so long as the gospel is being preached—from whatever motives on the part of the preachers: "Yes, and rejoice I will (*chairein*)" (Phil.1:18). The future tense of joy indicates that the Apostle's mood is no passing emotion but that it is one that will outlast all the present troubles; for it is connected with something that will remain necessary until the return of Jesus Christ, namely, the proclamation of the Christian gospel.

Not only does Paul speak of his own joy in this letter. He also writes of that of his readers and he encourages them in its continued manifestation. Since he believes that the church—including the congregation of Philippi—still requires his apostolic labours, he feels that the time for his departure "to be with Christ" (Phil.1:23) has not yet come. He knows that he will continue to help them forward and "add joy (*chara*) to your faith" (Phil.1:25). Faith here, as usually in Paul, stands for absolute trust in God as revealed to us by Jesus Christ. The Apostle assumes that joy is an essential element in that experience. Yet Paul's presence with the Philippian Christians will not only promote their joy in the faith. It will also give them ample cause for "unbounded pride (*kauchēma*) in Christ Jesus" (Phil.1:26).

The fact that Epaphroditus had fallen ill while he was with Paul had brought anxiety to the Philippians. Now that he was fully recovered, the Apostle was eager to send him back home in order that his friends may have "the happiness (*chairein*) of seeing him again" (Phil.2:28). He begs them to "welcome him then in the fellowship of the Lord with wholehearted delight (*chara*)" (Phil.2:29). Thus, even ordinary human relationships and friendships among Christians ought to be transfigured. They are given a certain sanctity on account of the fact that they are now "in the Lord".

At the beginning of chapter three, Paul appears to consider that he is coming to the close of his letter. He writes: "And now, friends, farewell: I wish you joy (*chairein*) in the Lord" (Phil.3:1). This farewell greeting is repeated in chapter four (Phil.4:4). Between these two imperatives, there is a section (probably extending from the middle of verse 1 to the end of verse 19) full of warnings against those perpetual enemies of Paul and of the true Christian faith, namely, the Judaizers. The Apostle emphasizes the fact that "we are the circumcised, we whose worship is spiritual, whose pride (*kauchasthai*) is in Christ Jesus, and who put no confidence in anything external" (Phil.3:3).

With the latter of these two imperatives of joy (Phil.4:4), Paul introduces a section of moral exhortation to his readers in such a way as to imply that their whole ethical behaviour should issue from the disposition of "joy in the Lord". The ideal is "to be sustained by the lofty sense of Christ's redemption, dispelling all anxiety and resolving into trust in God, and with its peace constituting the sure protection for the heart and mind."[14] The whole paragraph (Phil.4:4-7) is, as James Moffatt has pointed out[15], a "bright unity" and gives "an analysis of joy". The source of Paul's joy is always the redemption won for men by Jesus Christ. So it comes about that "joy in the Lord" is the most adequate way of summing up Paul's contribution to the Christian conception of joy. This buoyant attitude must assert itself against the realities of common life, both external and internal. As far as outward circumstances are concerned, we have to show forbearance in our dealings with other people, being content to consider them before ourselves. The supreme motive for such behaviour is the presence of Jesus Christ with the believer: "The Lord is near" (Phil.4:6). The companion danger is the inner one of worry and anxiety, through which, as Moffatt puts it, "the heart becomes its own torture-chamber". Against these two enemies, joy has to defend itself. It does so by "prayer for present need" and "gratitude for past aid"— "Have no anxiety, but in everything make your requests known to God in prayer and petition with thanksgiving" (Phil.4:6). There follows "the safety of joy" in the great assurance of the peace of God which guards our hearts and minds "in Christ Jesus". "The last words are not a pious phrase thrown in to close the verse, but the ground of that rare harmony of existence (*chara*) which is only, as it is always, conceivable and accessible through such a relationship. In this sympathy of life with life, every day comes to be a sort of festival: the enjoyment of life is not a strain, but a healthy energy; not a thing in the air, vague and emotional, made up from mood and circumstance, but vindicated as the natural temper and reasonable disposition of the heart. *En Kuriō ... en Christō*: the first and last word upon it is personal relationship. For, after all, what is the history of joy but simply the history of man's plain experience with his God in Jesus Christ?"[16]

Thus, from beginning to end, the keynote of the letter to the Philippians is one of joy. "Nowhere is the duty to celebrate in the midst of suffering more cogently stated."[17] The Apostle shows how, in spite of his present circumstances, he can still "rejoice in the Lord" and glory in work accomplished for his Master. Not only so; but he urges his readers to demonstrate the same exultant mood in their own lives, basing their inward feelings and their outward behaviour upon the joyful assurance of their redemption in Jesus Christ. The sum of the letter is indeed, as Bengel pointed out, "I rejoice, rejoice!"[18]

Citizens of Heaven

The abrupt change of tone and subject-matter in the middle of verse one of chapter three of the letter to the Philippians has led many scholars to believe that there is an interpolation here from another letter, though some still prefer to argue for the integrity of the whole letter. Whether or not there is an inter-polation, it is obvious that there is a change of subject-matter. Paul opens the chapter by saying: "And now, my friends, farewell; I wish you joy in the Lord." Then he appears to turn his attention towards his perpetual opponents, the Judaizers. Perhaps it was that at this point in his dictating of the letter he heard reports of havoc being wrought by these people and inserted a section in order to warn his readers. In that case, what follows would be in the nature of a parenthesis rather than an interpolation. Whichever of these two hypotheses we adopt, we have still to decide where Paul returns to his original theme of rejoicing—or, if we prefer, where the interpolation ends. Various opinions have been held on this subject.

Kirsopp Lake[19] argued for an interpolation extending from 3:1 (or 3:2) to 4:3. This would bring both imperatives of joy together. J. H. Michael, on the other hand, argued very convincingly that the interpolation closes at the end of verse 19.[20] In the best Greek manuscripts, verse 20 has *gar* (= for) as its second word. This follows on very naturally from the first half of verse 1: "And now, friends, farewell; I wish you joy in the Lord; for we are citizens of heaven." Paul is giving the reason for Christian joy. This reminds us of the words of Jesus on the return of the seventy-two: "Rejoice that your names are enrolled in heaven" (Lk.10:20). There are other hints that these words of Jesus are in Paul's mind. A few verses later, he mentions his fellow-workers, "whose names are in the book of life" (Phil.4:3). It is surely not without significance that the use of this phrase leads the Apostle to the repetition of the imperative for joy. Again, the emphasis on the expectation of our deliverer from heaven (Phil.3:20) may be due to the recollection of another statement of Jesus to the seventy-two: "I watched how Satan fell, like lightning, out of the sky" (Lk.10:18). From the same sky, Paul awaits his Saviour, the Lord Jesus Christ. All these points add up to quite an impressive argument at least for a parenthesis, if not for an interpolation, that closes at the end of verse 19. The resulting flow of thought is quite characteristic of Paul. Christian joy, finding its source in fellowship here and now with the risen Christ, has as its hope the perfection of all things in the heavenly kingdom. Though we live here on earth for a short period of time, our true homeland is with God, where we shall be made perfect at the last.

Paul's words to the Philippians can then be paraphrased as follows: "Finally, my friends, rejoice in the Lord. ... For we are citizens of heaven; our outlook goes beyond this world to the hopeful expectation of the Saviour, who will come from heaven, the Lord Jesus Christ. He will re-make these wretched bodies of ours to resemble his own glorious body, by that power of his which makes him the Master of everything that is."[21] Such is one aspect of the eschatological element that is involved in the Christian conception of joy according to the New Testament.

Pastoral Letters

The Pastoral Letters contain five examples of our vocabulary—two each in 1 Timothy and Titus and one in 2 Timothy.

The two instances in 1 Timothy are both of the adjective "blessed" (*makarios*) used as an epithet of God. The writer declares that he has been entrusted with "the gospel which tells of the glory of God *in his eternal felicity*" (1 Tim.1:11). His final charge to Timothy is that he should remain faithful to this gospel "until our Lord Jesus Christ appears" (1 Tim.6:14). This latter event will take place at the proper time through the intervention in history of "God who *in eternal felicity* alone holds sway" (1 Tim.6:15). These are the only two verses in the New Testament where the adjective is thus applied to God, after the manner of the use of the form *makar* in Homer. Yet "God's eternal felicity is not (after the Greek pattern) a self-regarding bliss."[22] He has already sent Jesus Christ into this world with the gospel of his love. Christians expect God to intervene again at the "second coming" of Christ in glory.

"Inward joy" (*chara*) appears once in 2 Timothy, where it is used of the joy of friendship. The writer declares that he longs to see Timothy "to make my happiness complete" (2 Tim.1:4). He desires to see his "fellow-worker" in order that he may have the joy of his company.

In the letter to Titus, "blessedness" (*makarios*) is found with reference to the Christian hope in the second coming of Christ. The life of purity to which we are called by the grace of God is sustained by "looking forward to the happy fulfilment of our hopes when the splendour of our great God and Saviour Christ Jesus will appear" (Titus 2:13). No longer are we "slaves to passions and pleasures (*hēdonē*) of every kind" (Titus 3:3). We have been saved through God's mercy and have thereby "in hope become heirs to eternal life'' (Tit.3:7). Thus we find the joyful eschatological hope of the Christian shining out in this letter to Titus.

18

THE THRESHOLD OF JOY — HEBREWS

There are seven instances of words for joy in the letter to the Hebrews. "Exultant joy" (*agalliasis*), unknown in the Pauline letters and found most often in Luke-Acts, occurs once. On the other hand, the characteristically Pauline idea of "joyful boasting" is hardly seen here—the sole example of the root being the noun *kauchēma*. "Courage" (*tharrein*) similarly appears once, while "inward joy" (*chara*) is used four times by the unknown author.

Exaltation of Christ and Exultation of Christians

In the doctrinal section of the letter (Heb.1:1-10:18), the writer proves the superiority of Jesus Christ to the angels (1:1-2:18), to Moses (3:1-4:13), and to Aaron (4:14-10:18). It is in the first two of these divisions that "exultant joy" and "boasting" are found—one in each.

One of the Old Testament passages quoted as proof of the pre-eminence of Christ over the angels declares that "thy God has set thee above thy fellows, by anointing with the oil of exultation" (Heb.1:9). Although the original reference in Psalm 45:7 is to the anointing of the king with festal oil, the author of Hebrews takes it as a messianic prophecy. He takes it as a reference to the ascension and exaltation of Christ to the supreme place in the universe above all angels on account of the fact that during his earthly life he "loved right and hated wrong" (Heb.1:9). Elsewhere, the author refers to Jesus as being "crowned with glory and honour" (Heb.2:9) and as having "taken his seat at the right hand of the throne of God" (Heb.12:2). It is worth noting that there is far more emphasis upon the exaltation of Christ in this letter than upon his resurrection, which is mentioned only once (Heb.13:20).

The superiority of Christ to Moses is taken to reside also in his unique relationship to God. Although Moses was faithful in God's house, it was in the capacity of a servant. Christ proved his fidelity in the same sphere as a son. We, as Christians, are members of God's house "if only we are fearless and keep our hope high"—literally, "keep the pride (*kauchēma*) of our hope" (Heb.3:6). "The author feels that in face of their temptations, their hope might grow faint. He therefore insists on their holding fast not simply a quietly cherished hope, but a loudly exulting, one might almost say aggressive, hope."[1]

Eschatological Assurance

At the opening of the practical section of the letter (Heb.10:19-13:25), the readers are exhorted to draw near to God "in sincerity of heart and full assurance of faith" (Heb.10:22), since Christ's death has given us glad confidence (*parrēsia*) in such an approach (Heb.10:19). After declaring that deliberate apostasy is unforgivable, the author encourages them in continued endurance by recalling their steadfastness in a time of persecution that is now past. "You shared the sufferings of the prisoners, and you cheerfully (*chara*) accepted the seizure of your possessions, knowing that you possessed something better and more lasting" (Heb.10:34).

Such eschatological assurance had also been part of the joy of Jesus. It was "for the sake of the joy that lay ahead of him" that he "endured the cross, making light of its disgrace" (Heb.12:2). We have already noted that an additional element as far as Jesus was concerned was the unselfish joy of self-sacrificing service and vicarious suffering.[2]

Although there has been a certain amount of persecution of Christians, the members of the church to which this letter is addressed have not yet resisted to the point of shedding their blood (Heb.12:4). Their struggle so far has not involved martyrdom, but can be called discipline inflicted upon them by God for their own good. Even though "discipline is never pleasant" (*chara*) at the time, when they look back upon their trials they will realize that they have been trained by them to be better Christians (Heb.12:11).

Joy in Christian Service

The final exhortations in the concluding chapter of the letter open with an appeal for religious living. Various Christian duties are summed up (Heb.13:1-6). Brotherly love, hospitality to strangers, the visiting of prisoners and other sufferers, and the sanctity of marriage are all insisted upon. Then the author emphasizes the need for a proper attitude to money and possessions in the light of God's promise to be with us. As a result, "we can take courage (*tharrein*) and say" that God is our helper (Heb.13:6).

Following upon this, there is a section dealing with church duties. This closes with the obligation of obedience to leaders, who "are tireless in their concern for you". This work ought to be to the leaders a source of joy as they see their labours bear fruit: "Let it be a happy task (*chara*) for them, and not pain and grief" (Heb.13:17). The author thus draws to a conclusion his appeal to his readers not to be "swept off your course by all sorts of outlandish teachings" (Heb.13:9). To do this would cause grief to their spiritual leaders and would bring no profit to themselves. Instead, they should submit to these men and give them real joy in their Christian service by showing them good results of their labours in the church.

Summary

The letter to the Hebrews emphasizes the eschatological element in the Christian conception of joy. Jesus himself endured his sufferings on account of the future joy that was laid up for him in heaven. This joy was fulfilled in his exaltation. Christians are called upon to follow his example in the glad assurance of the reality of the unseen world and of the promised eternal inheritance (Heb.9:15). "Live as always on the threshold of great joy."[3]

An additional element is present, however, in our author's conception of joy. Not only does he consider that the joy of Jesus contained an element of self-sacrificing service. He also emphasizes the joy that can be found by Christian leaders in their work in the church. They can rejoice when they see some measure of success accruing to their labours in the Christian lives being lived by those under them.

19

JOY IN SUFFERING — FIRST PETER

A good case can be made out for attributing 1 Peter (unlike 2 Peter) to Simon Peter, the fisherman from the Lake of Galilee, provided that we allow that Silvanus, otherwise known as Silas, was given a freer hand in its composition than is usually granted to an amanuensis. The date of its composition was probably around A.D.63/64, before the outbreak of the persecution of Christians by the Emperor Nero.

Suffering seems to have played no small part in the experience of the author, if not of the recipients as yet. He could have said what a more modern Christian said: "Our heavenly Father has led me through many dark places, but I have found out the truth of what good men have said. Some things, and these among the best, can only be seen when the lights of life are turned low, and the light of God is left to shine alone."[1]

The purpose of this letter was to encourage Christians in the northern part of Asia Minor to stand fast in their faith in time of trial. The Apostle does this by unfolding the ways of God as revealed in the gospel, by recalling the example of Christ himself, and by expounding the principles of conduct inherent in the Christian calling and baptism.

The keynote of the letter has been variously described as hope or Christian courage. These two ideas do play large parts in the message of the writer. The concept of joy in suffering also plays an important role. Words for joy appear no less than eight times within these four chapters. "Exultant joy" (*agallian*) is found in three different verses. "Inward joy" appears three times (*chara* once and *chairein* twice). Finally, there are two occurrences of the adjective "blessed" (*makarios*). Not only so; but Greek verbs meaning "to suffer" occur thirteen times (*paschein* twelve times and *lupein* once). As one writer has expressed it, "It seems as if the writer of 1 Peter has used the verb *paschō* (= I suffer), in relation to the sufferings of Christ and those which Christians have to bear, as a sort of Ariadne thread for his whole work."[2]

This co-existence of joy and suffering in 1 Peter has led some scholars to argue that it must originally have been composed as a baptismal and eucharistic service at Easter. Yet the paradox of joy in suffering found in it does not necessarily imply for it an Easter setting. Every Sunday is a weekly remembrance of the resurrection of Jesus Christ from the dead. We can account for the frequent allusions to suffering by recalling the purpose of the letter. It was written in order to encourage Christians to remain firm in their faith in face of possible persecution. They should be prepared to suffer just as Christ suffered. Yet he was able to rejoice even in his sufferings and through them he obtained final joy for himself as well as for others.

Joy in 1 Peter

The address and opening salutation are followed by a magnificent doxology containing "praise to God for the resurrection of Christ, and for the new life and new horizons opened thereby to Christians".[3] Such is the setting for the first passage concerning joy in suffering. It is on account of this eschatological hope that Christians can rejoice even amid trials of various kinds: "This is cause for great joy (*agallian*), even though you smart for a little while, if need be, under trials of many kinds" (1 Pet.1:6). The thought of the future inheritance kept for them in heaven can bring joy in the present world. Christians have the knowledge that whatever they have to endure is a means of probation. Moreover, what is genuine in their faith will be shown up as such at the time when Jesus Christ is revealed to men in his glory. Even though they cannot see Christ now, Christians nevertheless love him and believe in

him and "are transported (*agallian*) with a joy (*chara*) too great
for words" (1 Pet.1:8). This whole section has been called "the
paragraph of the broad panorama" since "it sparkles and
shimmers with joyful expectancy".[4]

Christ's beatitude on the persecuted (Mt.5:10) is echoed in
chapter three. The Apostle refers to the possibility of suffering:
"If you should suffer for your virtues, you may count yourselves happy (*makarios*)" (1 Pet.3:14). "If you should suffer" is
one of the few instances of the optative mood in the Greek New
Testament. Its use here suggests that suffering is a possibility,
not a certainty.

There is a final reference to joy in suffering in the last chapter
of 1 Peter. In this section, we see clearly that the letter was
addressed to Christians who were living under the shadow of
persecution that was liable to break out at any time. The
privilege of sharing Christ's sufferings is emphasized. Such is
the significance of enduring persecutions similar to those which
Christ experienced. Suffering for his sake, moreover, brings the
reward of bliss hereafter. This eschatological hope can help
Christians to rejoice here and now. "It gives you a share in
Christ's sufferings, and this is a cause for you (*chara*); and
when his glory is revealed, your joy (*chara*) will be triumphant
(*agallian*)" (1 Pet.4:13). Not only so; but they can thus obtain
the blessedness (*makarioi*) of the presence of the Holy Spirit
with them (1 Pet.4:14). This passage shows that even though the
doctrine of the Holy Spirit is less prominent in this letter than in
the Acts of the Apostles and elsewhere in the New Testament, it
was far from absent in Peter's theology. It was a presupposition
of his thought just as much as it was of that of Paul and other
Christian writers.

Summary

The paradox of joy in suffering thus runs through the whole of
this short letter. It comprises the main contribution of Peter to
the Christian conception of joy according to the New Testament.

Three elements can be clearly distinguished in this Petrine
concept. There is, first of all, the discipline of suffering. By
means of their trials and troubles, Christians are being tried just
as precious gold is tested by fire. Only what is true and genuine

in their faith will be able to survive such a process of proof (1 Pet.1:6-8).

Secondly, the Apostle stresses the privilege of suffering. By being persecuted for Christ's sake, Christians are sharing in his sufferings (1 Pet.4:13).

Finally, there is the reward of suffering in the next world. The joy of Christians will be triumphant at the revelation of Christ's glory (1 Pet.1:6-8; 4:13). "In the certainty that good and evil will alike be judged, Christians who suffer for their faith are exhorted to commit themselves into God's hands in well-doing."[5]

20

THE JOY OF PRACTICAL CHRISTIANITY — JAMES

In spite of Martin Luther's low opinion of this letter—"a right strawy epistle with no tang of the gospel about it"—there are many interesting and valuable things here, including several references to various aspects of the Christian conception of joy. It is *par excellence* the letter of Christian practice. We can therefore characterize its contribution to our present subject as "the joy of practical Christianity".

In all, there are fourteen examples of words for joy in this short letter. "Inward joy" appears three times (*chairein* once and *chara* twice), "blessedness" three times (*makarios* twice and *makarizein* once), "boasting" five times (*kauchasthai* twice, *katakauchasthai* twice and *kauchēsis* once), "pleasure" (*hēdonē*) twice, and "optimism" (*euthumein*) once. In our study of these, we shall group them together by subject-matter under the heading of the five sermonettes that can be picked out of the letter by re-arranging the material.[1] The author deals, rather haphazardly, with these five main subjects of practical Christianity. In four out of five of his sermons, James has something to say about joy. The five themes found in this letter are as follows:

(1) Trials and temptations—Jas.1:2-8, 12-18;

(2) Rich man and poor—Jas.1:9-11; 4:8-10,13-16; 5:1-6; 2:1-13;

(3) Faith and works—Jas.1:19-25,27; 2:14-26; 4:17; 3:13-18; 4:1-7;

(4) The tongue—Jas.1:26; 3:1-12; 4:11-12; 5:12;

(5) Patience and prayer—Jas.5:7-11, 13-20.

We shall examine the first three and the last of these five themes in turn.

Trials and Temptations

After the opening verse, in which the infinitive *chairein* is used as a greeting (Jas.1:1), James turns immediately to the question of trials and temptations. He suggests that Christians can even "welcome (*chara*) them as friends" (Jas 1:2—JBP). The reason given in the next verse—"such testing of your faith breeds fortitude" (Jas.1:3)—reminds us of Peter's analogy with gold which "passes through the assayer's fire (1 Pet.1:7). Both writers are trying to encourage their readers in difficult times by referring them to the disciplinary effect that suffering has upon character. Paul was also aware that "suffering trains us to endure" (Rom.5:3) and could even exult (*kauchasthai*) in it.

James repeats the idea a few verses later with the use of the adjective *makarios*. He adds to the concept the notion of the reward of suffering—also familiar to us from 1 Peter: "Happy the man who remains steadfast under trial, for having passed that test he will receive for his prize the gift of life promised to those who love God" (Jas.1:12). Devotion to God, which has been proved genuine through the endurance of trial, will be rewarded hereafter by the gift of life that is crowned with joy. A victorious athlete who has persevered through all difficulties wins the coveted prize. Similarly, a glorious reward is promised in this beatitude on endurance. There is a parallel in the saying of Jesus: "The man who holds out to the end will be saved" (Mk.13:13).

Rich Man and Poor

James emphasizes the equality of the rich man and the poor, first of all in the face of death. This is somewhat in the style of Shirley's poem, *Death the Leveller:*

The glories of our blood and state
    Are shadows, not substantial things;

> There is no armour against fate;
>   Death lays his icy hand on kings;
>   Sceptre and crown
>   Must tumble down,
> And in the dust be equal made
> With the poor crooked scythe and spade.[2]

Since both are thus on the same level, the poor man is exalted by death while the rich man is brought low: "The brother in humble circumstances may well be proud (*kauchasthai*) that God lifts him up ..." (Jas.1:9).

Similarly, rich and poor alike are called to seek God's pardon in penitence since all have sinned: "Come close to God ... make your hands clean ... be sorrowful, mourn and weep. Turn your laughter into mourning and your gaiety (*chara*) into gloom" (Jas.4:8f.). "For an Oriental, fasting and lamentation were the spontaneous and natural expression of deep sorrow. Our Lord permits but never prescribes it, only insisting that it must be absolutely sincere and not for show (Mt.6:16ff.)."[3] James, however, seems to go one step further than Jesus in demanding these outward signs of repentance for rich and poor alike. Joy in worship appears to have played little or no part in his scheme of thinking, overwhelmed as he was by the enormity of sin. While the poor are by no means faultless, James has a special word of denunciation for the vices of the rich after the manner of the Old Testament prophets (Jas.4:13-16; 5:1-6). In all their business of planning, they forget to take God into account. In spite of their pride in the Law, they fail to do right. As a result, they only boast in their ignorance. "All such boasting (*kauchēsis*) is wrong" (Jas.4:16).

In view of the equality of men as sinners before God and in the face of death, James calls his readers to show Christian impartiality in their dealings with different classes of society (Jas.2:1-13). This section closes with an echo of Christ's beatitude on the merciful. After advising Christians "always to speak and act as men who are to be judged under a law of freedom" (Jas.2:12), the author gives the reason for such conduct. God will show mercy to those who have exercised a like quality in their dealings with other people. "Mercy triumphs over (*katakauchasthai*) judgement" (Jas.2:13).

Faith and Works

The favourite theme of the letter of James is that of faith and works. For James, faith means religious belief or creed. He argues that true Christian faith will be known on account of the practical Christianity to which it gives rise. Faith without works is dead. In this connection, the closing remarks of the Sermon on the Mount (Mt.7:24-27) are echoed. The man who looks closely into the perfect law and acts upon it "is the man who by acting will find happiness (*makarios*)" (Jas.1:25). If any are harbouring "bitter jealousy and selfish ambition" in their hearts, they should not let these manifest themselves in outward deeds: "Do not boast (*katakauchasthai*) and be false to the truth" (Jas.3:14—RSV).

The bitter jealousy and selfish ambition in the hearts of his Jewish readers appear to be in the mind of James again at the beginning of chapter four, when he asks the cause of fightings amongst them. He answers his own question by asking another: "Do they not spring from the aggressiveness of your bodily desires (*hēdonē*)?" (Jas.4:1; cf.Jas.4:3). Party strife and quarrelsomeness poisoned many Jewish communities. James maintains that such "faction fights are the logical outcome of unbridled passions".[4]

Patience and Prayer

In chapter five, we find the sermonette on patience and prayer. The readers are exhorted to "be patient ... until the Lord comes" (Jas.5:7). They are given as examples to follow people in the Old Testament who persisted in their trust in God in spite of adverse circumstances. "We count them happy (*makarizein*) who stood firm" (Jas.5:11). Job, whose steadfastness is referred to, remained faithful to God even when things seemed to be going against him. To the Christian, as to the Jewish prophets of old, two aids to such devotion and loyalty are available—prayer and praise. "Is anyone among you in trouble? He should turn to prayer. Is anyone in good heart (*euthumein*)? He should sing praises" (Jas.5:13).

Summary

The letter of James thus stresses the possibility and even the duty of joy in the midst of trials and temptations, the faithful endurance of which earns a reward in the life to come. The doctrine of the equality of men as sinners and as mortal beings gives rise not only to the paradox of boasting in faith and humility before God. It also leads to the call for impartiality in the dealings of Christians with rich and poor alike. As they practise mercy upon others, so will they be granted mercy by God. The person who is not only a hearer of the word but also a doer will be blessed. The joy of such practical Christianity is inspired by prayer and praise—prayer that is most essential in time of suffering and praise that flows from optimism, the mood of Christian faith.

21

THE JOY OF THE REDEEMED — REVELATION

The Book of Revelation was probably written towards the close of the first century A.D. at a time of great crisis for the Christian Church.[1] After the great fire of Rome in A.D.64, Nero had caused suspicion to rest upon the new religion by fostering responsibility for the disaster upon Christians. Many of them were put to death in the ensuing "killing time". Organized persecution, however, did not break out till the reign of the Emperor Domitian, who tried to unify the Roman Empire by means of emperor worship. He caused an edict to be issued throughout his dominions. Divine honours were to be paid to himself alone. Little resistance was offered to this new cult by the majority of Rome's subjects. Christians, however, regarded it with horror.

Thus began the conflict between the state and the church that was to last for two centuries. It ended with Constantine's acceptance of Christianity as the state religion. It was to meet the trials of the persecution in the closing years of the first century A.D. that this book was written by John the Seer.[2] The author had himself been banished to the island of Patmos in the Aegean Sea on account of his witness to Christ.

Though composed at such a critical period in the history of the Christian church, Revelation is by no means a pessimistic

piece of writing. John the Seer declares his firm belief in the
ultimate victory of good and points his readers away from the
perils and persecutions of earth to the joy of the redeemed in
heaven. No fewer than thirteen times do we find examples of
cognates and synonyms for joy in this book. Seven of these are
beatitudes introduced by the adjective "blessed" (*makarios*),
while "inward joy" (*chairein*) occurs twice, "gladness" (euphrainesthai) three times, and "exultant joy" (*agallian*) once.

Present Persecution

The whole prophecy is framed within promises of blessing
upon those who listen to it. These are in the form of beatitudes
introduced by *makarios* (Rev.1:3; 22:7). The reason behind the
assurance of happiness is the imminence of the coming of
Christ.

The writer of Revelation, however, is not a thoughtless opti-
mist who tries to persuade his readers that everything will turn
out right tomorrow. Rather does he see in the existing troubles
the precursors of many more. He warns Christians to expect a
period of world-wide sorrow and desolation. They must be
prepared for martyrdom and must take courage in the face of
death.

The temporary triumph of evil is depicted in the rejoicing of
the inhabitants of the earth over the defeat of the two prophets
whose testimony had troubled their consciences: "All men on
earth gloat (*chairein*) over them, make merry (*euphrainesthai*),
and exchange presents" (Rev.11:10). Each of the three verbs
used adds something to the festive picture. *Chairein* describes
the inner state that gives rise to the merry-making, while the
exuberant joy of the earth-dwellers is shown by the fact that
presents are given and received.

Ultimate Victory

The victory of evil is short-lived, however, and the two
prophets are vindicated by God in their resurrection from the
dead and in their assumption into heaven in the sight of their
foes (Rev.11:11ff.). In this way, the writer of the apocalypse
gives expression to his conviction that death is not a final and
irrevocable calamity. There is something more valuable even

than life itself in its earthly form. The joy of materialistic pleasures disappears with the passing of this world of space and
time, whereas the joy of the redeemed is eternal.

The struggle on earth is matched by the war in heaven
between Michael and his angels on the one side and the devil
and his angels on the other. Here again, victory rests with the
good and not with the evil. Heaven and its inhabitants are called
upon to take part in the eschatological joy that follows upon the
defeat of the devil (Rev.12:12—*euphrainesthai*).

The blessedness of the redeemed is referred to in the beatitude
on the dead that John was commanded to write by the voice
from heaven: "Happy (*makarios*) are the dead who die in the
faith of Christ" (Rev.14:13). Their happiness is defined in the
confirmatory statement made by the Spirit: "Happy indeed are
they: let them rest from their labours, for their deeds follow
them."[3] Patient endurance of suffering upon earth is rewarded
hereafter by the restful joy of heaven that is to be attained by all
who "die in the faith of Christ".

Another beatitude is inserted into the record of doom in
chapter sixteen. A word of comfort and exhortation is given to
Christians: "That is the day when I come like a thief! Happy
(*makarios*) the man who stays awake and keeps on his clothes,
so that he will not have to go naked and ashamed for all to see"
(Rev.16:15). This is modelled upon such a saying of Christ's as
that found at the close of the parable of the bridesmaids
(Mt.25:13). The doctrine of the second coming of Christ is both
a call to Christians to watchfulness and also a promise of joy to
the faithful. In addition, of course, it contains an element of
warning to those who lapse from the Christian way.

Chapter eighteen contains a long description of the gloom
and desolation of the defeated city of Babylon (standing for
Rome). It reaches its climax in the summons to joy over the
conquered enemy: "Let heaven exult over (*euphrainein*) her;
exult, apostles and prophets and people of God; for in the
judgement against her he has vindicated your cause" (Rev.
18:20). In contrast to the dark picture of earthly destruction, the
scene of triumph in heaven is painted for us in the following
chapter. This opens with a description of the marriage of the
Lamb (Rev.19:1-10)—a common eschatological symbol in the
New Testament and one that gives a true picture of the joy of

heaven. The full extent of the feeling of triumphant rejoicing is indicated by the fourfold use of the exclamation "Hallelujah!" in the glorious songs of heaven. The word occurs nowhere else in the New Testament, thus being reserved for the heavenly choirs. The final and most magnificent of the hallelujah choruses, the opening of which is made use of by Handel in his *Messiah*, contains the joyful thanksgiving and praise of the redeemed: "Exult (*chairein*) and shout for joy (*agallian*) and do him homage, for the wedding-day of the Lamb has come" (Rev. 19:7). The joyful exultation of this great multitude in heaven moves the angel to command John to write another beatitude: "Happy (*makarios*) are those who are invited to the wedding-supper of the Lamb" (Rev.19:9).

Two remaining beatitudes further describe the joy of the redeemed. In his account of the concept of the millennium, John declares that only those who have suffered martyrdom for their faith will share in the first resurrection. All others have to wait till the completion of a thousand years. As a result, he declares: "Happy (*makarios*) indeed, and one of God's own people, is the man who shares in this first resurrection" (Rev. 20:6). Such people escape "the second death" and reign instead with Christ as priests of God.

Finally, in the epilogue to the whole book, there is another beatitude on the redeemed in heaven: "Happy (*makarios*) are those who wash their robes clean! They will have the right to the tree of life and will enter by the gates of the city" (Rev.22:14). The tree of life and entering the city by the gates are attempts to describe the joy of the redeemed. They are the reward given to "those who wash their robes clean".

Summary

The writer of the Book of Revelation declares that the joy of the opponents of Christianity is short-lived. In the end, victory will rest with God. His philosophy of history is similar to that of Lowell:

> Though the cause of Evil prosper, yet 'tis Truth alone is
> strong ...
> Truth for ever on the scaffold, Wrong for ever on the
> throne—

Yet that scaffold sways the Future, and, behind the dim
   unknown,
   Standeth God within the shadow, keeping watch above
   His own.

John the Seer describes heaven and its inhabitants as being
summoned to share in the eschatological joy of the final victory.
In contrast to the ephemeral festivities of materialistic earth-
dwellers, the joy of the redeemed is eternal. It is depicted in
various symbolic pictures. Having endured steadfastly to the
end and having died in the faith of Christ, they rest from their
labours and share in the marriage supper of the Lamb. Thus
does John attempt to describe the inexpressible joy of the redeemed and to give us a glimpse of the glories of the invisible
world.

22

CONCLUSION — WE JOY IN GOD[1]

Our examination of the variety of words for joy and of the heritage of joy that we find in individual authors has shown how widespread this idea is in the New Testament. In fact, as one writer, has put it, "Joy is more conspicuous in Christianity than in any other religion and in the Bible than in any other literature."[2]

From beginning to end, the message of the New Testament is one of joy; for it declares the "good news" of the Christian gospel. Jesus himself is the supreme example for us to follow in this respect, as in other ways, too. He was indeed "the Man of Joy". It is, therefore, only to be expected that "from the Annunciation to the Ascension the note of joy abounds in the Gospel accounts".[3] This is particularly true of Luke's Gospel, which is the gospel of joy *par excellence.*

Our Heritage of Joy

Each of the New Testament writers, almost without exception, has some contribution to make to the Christian conception of joy. While Luke in his gospel shows the joy of Jesus, in the Acts of the Apostles he describes the ever-widening circle of joy in the early Church. John emphasizes the fulness of joy that Jesus wished for his followers.

The Apostle Paul stresses the true basis of the joy of the Christian in his relationship with his risen Lord and in the fellowship of the Christian church. Since the phrase "in Christ" appears very frequently in his correspondence and epitomizes his whole Christian experience, we can sum up his contribution to our present subject of study as "joy in the Lord".

The joy that seeks us through pain and suffering, to adapt words of the blind Scottish minister and hymn-writer George Matheson[4], is found especially in the letter written by the Apostle Peter to Christians in Asia Minor; but is also apparent in the letter of Christian practice sent by the Apostle James to "the Twelve Tribes dispersed throughout the world" (Jas.1:1). Eschatological joy is shown in particular in the "short exhortation" (Heb.13:22) of the unknown writer of the letter to the Hebrews. It is also seen in John the Seer's description of the joy of the redeemed in heaven.

Theological Foundations

A close study of the occurrences of words for joy in the New Testament reveals that the Christian conception of joy is firmly based on the main doctrines of the Christian faith. It is founded on the very character of God as Father. Though in his teaching about the fatherhood of God Jesus was drawing to a certain extent upon Jewish doctrine, he went beyond current practice by daring to call God by the familiar term *Abba*—or "Daddy" as a child might say today. Jesus stressed God's providential and individual care of each individual. The joy that comes through the forgiveness of sins and through the finished work of Christ on the cross is central to the Christian understanding of the atonement. Our reconciliation to God the Father was accomplished by Jesus Christ through his death and resurrection.

Christian joy, which is founded on the very character of God, is also based on the historical events of the incarnation, the resurrection and the exaltation of Christ. In fact, the joy of Christianity can be said to revolve round the great festivals of the Christian year. The first of these and the one on which all the others ultimately depend is the festival of the incarnation celebrated at the Christmas season. Equally important, however, is the joy associated with Easter; for it is only in virtue of the resurrection that there is such a thing as the Christian conception of joy. Only because Jesus Christ was raised from the dead by God can we consider joy as one of the main constituents of our religion.

Christian joy is also connected with the experience and the doctrine of the Holy Spirit. It depends on the present indwelling of God in the heart of the Christian believer. As Principal Rainy put it, "Joy is the flag which is flown from the castle of the heart when the King is in residence there."[5] Similarly, Adamnan wrote in his life of St. Columba: "He was dear to everybody, always showed a cheerful face, and in his inmost heart was made glad with the joy of the Holy Spirit."[6]

Practical Implications

So much for the "Why?" of Christian joy. What about the "How?" It is quite clear that "the New Testament has a message for modern man in its emphasis on joy".[7] In other words, the fact that the New Testament is the most joyful book in the world, the fact that nearly every New Testament writer emphasizes at least one aspect of this Christian concept, and the fact that the joy of Christianity is firmly based on the great doctrines of the faith must have implications for us today. There are, or should be, tremendous consequences of all this for Christian life and work, worship and service in the world in this and in every generation.

Christian joy, first of all, should find expression in revitalized worship; for we sing for joy. Again, it affects our daily life and work in the world as well as our public worship of God on Sundays. For the Christian, pain and suffering are transformed, while service for others is given a new dimension; for we live for Christ and rejoice in his service.

Finally, Christians should always live as on the threshold of great joy; for we die to live. We can rejoice at all times in the hope of our eternal glory, through Jesus Christ our Lord. So, "the Christian faith is not a dirge but a paean of joy".[8] Or, as St. Francis of Assisi expressed it, "Let us leave sadness to the devil and his angels. As for us, what can we be but rejoicing and glad?"

Abbreviations used in Notes

AG   Bauer's *Greek-English Lexicon of the New Testament* translated by W.F. Arndt and F.W. Gingrich, Cambridge University Press 1957.

AV   Authorised Version of the Bible

BLNTG   Cremer's *Biblico-Theological Lexicon of New Testament Greek* translated by W. Urwick, T. & T. Clark 1886.

DNTT   The New International *Dictionary of New Testament Theology* edited by C. Brown, The Paternoster Press 1975-1978.

EGT   *Expositor's Greek Testament* edited by J. Hastings, Hodder & Stoughton 1904.

EONT   Matthew Henry, *An Exposition of the Old and New Testament* (9 vols), J. Nisbet and Co. 1721.

ET   *The Expository Times* founded by J. Hastings, T. & T. Clark.

Exp.   *The Expositor* edited by W.R. Nicoll, Hodder & Stoughton 1874-1924.

GNT   D.J.A. Bengel, *Gnomon Novi Testamenti* (3rd edition), D. Nutt, Williams & Norgate; Macmillan & Co. 1855.

HDB(1)   J. Hastings, *Dictionary of the Bible* (1 vol.), T. & T. Clark 1909.

HDB(5)   J. Hastings, *Dictionary of the Bible* (5 vols), T. & T. Clark 1898-1904.

JBL   *Journal of Biblical Literature* published quarterly by the Society of Biblical Literature.

JBP   J.B. Phillips, *Letters to Young Churches*, G.Bles 1947.

JM   J. Moffatt, *A New Translation of the Bible*, Hodder & Stoughton 1950.

LCL   *Loeb Classical Library* edited by T.E. Page, E. Capps, W.H.D. Rouse; London, W. Heinemann.

LS   H.G. Liddell and R. Scott, *A Greek-English Lexicon*, Clarendon Press.

NEB   The *New English Bible*, Oxford University Press/
         Cambridge University Press 1970.
RSV   The *Revised Standard Version*, Nelson and Sons 1952.
RVUV   *Religionsgeschichtliche Versuche und Vorarbeiten* edited
         by R. Wünsch and L. Deubner, Giessen, A. Töpelmann.
STT   *Suomalaisen   Tiedeakatemian   Toimituksia*—Annales
         Academiae Scientiarum Fennicae, Helsinki vol. 26 (1932)
         and vol. 37 (1937).
TBT   *The Bible Translator* edited by P. Ellingworth, United
         Bible Societies.
TDNT   *Theological Dictionary of the New Testament* edited by G.
         Kittel and translated by G.W. Bromiley (10 vols), Wm B.
         Eerdmans Publishing Company 1964-1976.
TWNT   *Theologisches Wörterbuch zum Neuen Testament* edited
         by G. Kittel, Stuttgart, W. Kohlhammer 1933 on.
VGT   J.H. Moulton and G. Milligan, *The Vocabulary of the
         Greek New Testament* illustrated from the papyri and
         other non-literary sources, Hodder & Stoughton 1930.

NOTES

INTRODUCTION
(Pages 11—15)

1. E. Bevan, *Hellenism and Christianity* (George Allen and Unwin 1921), p.72.
2. G. H. Box, "Early Christianity and the Hellenic World" in Exp.9.2.138.
3. M. Jones, "The Hellenistic World behind the New Testament" in Exp.8.21.358.
4. T. Mommsen, *The History of Rome*—translated by W. P. Dickson (R. Bentley and Son 1875), 4.2.619.
5. J. M. Murry, *The Life of Christ* (Jonathan Cape 1926), p.64.
6. M. Arnold, *Lyric, Dramatic, and Elegiac Poems* (Macmillan 1881), vol.2, p.297ff.
7. W. G. Morrice, *We Joy in God* (S.P.C.K. 1977).

CHAPTER 1
(Pages 19—24)

1. Cf. BLNTG 590.
2. Cf. R. Bultmann in TDNT 1.19: "The meaning of the word is the cultic joy which celebrates and extols the help and acts of God, whether shown to the people or community or to the individual."
3. *Ibid.*, p.20; cf. *infra*, p.137.
4. So GNT 862.
5. See W. G. Morrice, *op.cit.*, chapter 5—*We Sing for Joy*. This note of joy in worship has been a characteristic of the modern charismatic movement and of Pentecostalists. Cf. W. J. Hollenweger's description of a Pentecostalist service: "The congregation clapped their hands in time with the tunes and ventilated their joy in spontaneous testimony" (*The Pentecostals*, SCM Press 1972, p.3). Cf. also K. Barth, *Church Dogmatics* (T. & T. Clark 1936-69), editors G. W. Bromiley and T. F. Torrance, 3.4.68f.: "If we remember that joy in God is something high and rare—*res severa verum gaudium*—we shall always have to say that it is in every respect an infallible criterion of Sabbath observance whether and how sincerely we are in a position to celebrate it as a true day of joy. ... The Church must not allow itself to become dull, nor its services dark and gloomy. ... How otherwise has it the right to complain at the mass of counterfeit joy which disfigures this day?"

CHAPTER 2
(Pages 25—26)

1. From a shipmate's letter quoted by G. Seaver, *Edward Wilson of the Antarctic: naturalist and friend* (John Murray 1933), p.209.

CHAPTER 3
(Pages 27—32)

1. See H. A. A. Kennedy, *Sources of New Testament Greek* (T. & T. Clark 1895), p.155.
2. A. B. Bruce, EGT ii 558.
3. GNT p.447.
4. EGT ii 86.
5. EGT iv 182.
6. For examples, see VGT p.267.

CHAPTER 4
(Pages 33—37)

1. VGT p.277.
2. "Joy" here is *chara*—see Chapter Ten.
3. EONT vii 187.
4. Robert Burns.

CHAPTER 5
(Pages 38—44)

1. Paris Papyri 51.19 (160 B.C.)—VGT p.284.
2. Cf. TWNT/TDNT 3.26f.
3. Cf. J. H. Bernard, *The Gospel according to St John* (T. & T. Clark 1928), vol.2, p.524.
4. G. Seaver, *op.cit.*, p.xi.

CHAPTER 6
(Pages 45—48)

1. See TDNT 3.297.
2. VGT p.303.
3. TWNT 3.299/TDNT 3.298.
4. EGT ii 691.

CHAPTER 7
(Pages 49—55)

1. LS *in loco*.
2. Stobaeus: *Ecloge* 3.127.9; TWNT 3.646.
3. See TWNT 3.647f.; cf. DNTT 227.
4. Cf. C. E. B. Cranfield, *The Epistle to the Romans* (T. & T. Clark 1975), vol.1, p.165: "The use of this word-group in the NT is almost exclusively Pauline."
5. Cf. HDB(5) 2.790.
6. Cf. C. E. B. Cranfield, *op.cit.*, p.170, who argues that in Rom.2:23 the verb *kauchasthai* is not being used simply in a bad sense. "The Jew ought

to boast in the law, but the truth is that his actual boasting in the law is to a very large extent the wrong sort of boasting in the law."

CHAPTER 8
(Pages 56—64)

1. See TDNT 4.363f.
2. See G. L. Dirichlet, "De Veterum Macarismis" in RVUV vol.14 (1914), p.28f.
3. Menander, *Fragments from Unidentified Plays*—"The Brothers": LCL p.312f.
4. Pindar, *Olympic Odes* 8.11: LCL p.70f.
5. Euripides, *Bacchae* 72-75, as translated by E. R. Dodds, *Euripides Bacchae* (Oxford University Press 1960), p.75, who comments: "Such formulas of beatitude are traditional in Greek poetry."
6. Cf. TDNT 4.367.
7. A. Plummer, *The Gospel according to St Luke* (T. & T. Clark 1896), p.30; cf. W. Grundmann, *Das Evangelium nach Lukas* (Berlin 1966), p.62; I. H. Marshall, *The Gospel of Luke* (Paternoster Press 1978), p.82.
8. C. G. Montefiore, *The Synoptic Gospels* (Macmillan & Co. 1927), vol.2, p.476.
9. T. W. Manson, *The Sayings of Jesus* (SCM Press 1949), p.47; cf. C. C. McCown in "The Beatitudes in the Light of Ancient Ideals"—JBL 46 (1927), pp.50-61, who argues that the authenticity of Luke's versions of these beatitudes is confirmed by considering the demand for social justice among both Jews and non-Jews in the ancient world. Spiritualizing interpretations of the beatitudes, of which the first was Matthew's, are clearly mistaken. Jesus taught that "the wrongs and injustices that flowed from the oppression and pride of the rich and powerful must cease when God reigned on earth".
10. I. H. Marshall, *op.cit.*, p.249.
11. See C. G. Montefiore, *Rabbinic Literature and Gospel Teachings* (Macmillan & Co. 1930), p.27ff.
12. J. H. Bernard, *The Gospel according to St John* (T. & T. Clark 1928), p.467.
13. My own translation, which is an emendation of NEB. It seems to me that the clause, "let them rest from their labours", makes better sense taken thus as an example of the imperatival *hina* (as in JM) rather than as an adverbial clause of purpose. It states the nature of the reward offered to martyrs on account of their patient endurance in time of suffering. See my article on "The Imperatival *hina*" in TBT vol.23 (1972), pp.326-330. Cf. N. Turner, *Grammatical Insights into the New Testament* (T. & T. Clark 1965), p.48; also N. Turner in J. H. Moulton, *A Grammar of New Testament Greek*, vol.4 (T. & T. Clark 1976), p.151.
14. Here again there may be an imperatival *hina*.

CHAPTER 9
(Pages 65—67)

1. Cf. TDNT 7.402.
2. See A. Plummer, *op.cit.*, p.28.
3. Quoted by A. B. Davidson, *The Called of God*—Selected Sermons edited by J. A. Paterson (T. & T. Clark 1902), p.30.

CHAPTER 10
(Pages 68—75)

1. Karl Barth (*op.cit.*, 3.4.378) shows that the connection between "grace" and "joy" operates in the other direction also. "To be joyful is to expect that life will reveal itself as God's gift of grace. ... To be joyful means to look out for opportunities of gratitude."
2. A. S. Hunt and C. C. Edgar, *Select Papyri*—LCL vol.1, p.26f.
3. VGT 682.
4. TDNT 9.366.
5. See J. H. Moulton, *A Grammar of New Testament Greek*, vol.1 (T. & T. Clark 1906), p.179; cf. GNT 593: "Infinitivus pro imperativo, Graecis non infrequens, et his moratus."
6. Cf. C. K. Barrett, *The Second Epistle to the Corinthians* (A. & C. Black 1973), p.342, who translates, "Finally, brothers, goodbye."
7. R. Bultmann, *The Theology of the New Testament* (SCM Press 1952), vol.1, p.339.
8. See J. Jeremias, *The Parables of Jesus* (SCM Press 1963), p.200f.; cf. E. G. Gulin, *Die Freude im Neuen Testament* (1 Teil) in STT 26 (1932), p.37.
9. See H. Montefiore and H. E. W. Turner, *Thomas and the Evangelists* (SCM Press 1962), p.66.
10. Cf. DNTT 2.357.

CHAPTER 11
(Pages 76—78)

1. VGT 616.
2. Moulton and Milligan in Exp.8.1.568.
3. A. E. Whitham, *The Pastures of his Presence* (Hodder & Stoughton 1939), p.197.
4. K. Barth, *op.cit.*, 3.4.380.
5. Cf. E. G. Gulin in STT 37 (1937), p.276: "Es ist die Gemeinschaft 'im Herrn', die hier überall die rein 'soziale' Freude vertieft und ihr ein neues Daseinsrecht verbürgt."

CHAPTER 12
(Pages 79—81)

1. Lewis Carroll, *Through the Looking Glass*.
2. See W. G. Morrice, *We Joy in God*, p.61f.
3. J. Denney, *Studies in Theology* (Hodder & Stoughton 1895), p.171.

CHAPTER 13
(Pages 85—90)

1. E. Renan, *The Life of Christ* (Trübner & Co. 1864), p.149.
2. Cf. J. Moffatt, "What was the Joy of Jesus?" in Exp.8.22.114.
3. For this whole section, see W. G. Morrice, *The New Beginning* (The Saint Andrew Press 1981), p.60.
4. Born in Annan in Dumfriesshire in 1792, Edward Irving was a Church of Scotland minister in London until deposed by the Presbytery. His followers constituted themselves as the "Catholic Apostolic Church". See his biography written by Mrs Oliphant and published in London by Hurst and Blackett in two volumes in 1862.

CHAPTER 14
(Pages 91—99)

1. A. Harnack, *Luke the Physician*—translated by W. D. Morrison (Williams & Norgate 1907), p.163f.
2. See *supra*, pp.64,67.
3. W. Alexander, *The Leading Ideas of the Gospels* (Macmillan & Co. 1892), p.157.
4. W. F. Adeney, *St. Luke* (T. C. & E. C. Jack 1901), p.8.
5. GNT 482.
6. A. M. Hunter, *Introducing the New Testament* (SCM Press 2nd ed. 1957), p.70.

CHAPTER 15
(Pages 100—104)

1. "Carpus" in Exp. 1.1.82.
2. C. G. Montefiore, *Rabbinic Literature and Gospel Teachings* (Macmillan and Co. 1930), p.1.
3. J. Jeremias, *The Parables of Jesus*, p.201.
4. *The Gospel according to Thomas*—Coptic Text established and translated by A. Guillaumont, H.-Ch. Puech, G. Quispel, W. Till and Yasah 'Abd Al Masih (Brill and Collins, 1959), p.55.
5. A. M. Hunter, *Interpreting the Parables* (S.C.M. 1960), p.60.
6. J. Jeremias, *op.cit.*, p.40; A. M. Hunter, *op.cit.*, p.6.
7. So J. Jeremias, *The Eucharistic Words of Jesus* (Blackwell 1955), p.156, following G. Dalman, *Worte Jesus*, p.96.
8. EGT 1.336.
9. J. Jeremias, *The Parables of Jesus*, p.180.
10. *Ibid.*, p.174f.

CHAPTER 16
(Pages 105—110)

1. See E. C. Hoskyns, *The Fourth Gospel* (Faber & Faber 1940), vol.1, p.249.

2. See C. K. Barrett, *The Gospel according to St John* (S.P.C.K. 1978), p.265.
3. See *supra*, p.14.
4. See J. H. Bernard, *St John*—I.C.C. (T. & T. Clark 1928), vol.2, p.321.
5. J. Jeremias, *The Parables of Jesus*, p.219.
6. W. Temple, *Readings in St John's Gospel* (Macmillan & Co. 1950), p.295f.
7. Cf. C. K. Barrett, *op.cit.*, p.223.
8. Swete—as quoted by E. C. Hoskyns, *op.cit.*, p.578f.
9. W. F. Howard, *Christianity according to St John* (Duckworth 1943), p.135f.
10. J. H. Bernard, *op.cit.*, vol.2, p.380.

CHAPTER 17
(Pages 111—133)

1. The Pauline authorship of the letter to the Ephesians is disputed by some scholars. See, e.g., C. L. Mitton, *The Epistle to the Ephesians: its Authorship, Origin and Purpose* (Clarendon Press 1951) and *Ephesians* (Oliphants 1976). Cf. J. Knox, *Chapters in a Life of Paul* (Abingdon Press), p.20f.
2. See P. N. Harrison, *The Problem of the Pastorals* (Oxford University Press 1921); cf. A. T. Hanson, *Studies in the Pastoral Epistles* (S.P.C.K. 1968), p.120: "If they are Pauline, they represent a dismal conclusion to Paul's writings; if they are post-Pauline, they are an admirable and indispensable illustration of the state of the Church at the end of the first century."
3. The Greek word for grace (*charis*) is from the same root as the word for inward joy (*chara*). See *supra*, pp.64,67. It is of interest that 88 out of the 154 occurrences of *charis* in the New Testament are in Paul's letters, i.e., 57%.
4. I accept the South Galatian view propounded by Sir William Ramsay that the recipients of this letter were the members of the churches founded by Paul in the course of his first journey.
5. G. P. Wiles, *Paul's Intercessory Prayers* (Cambridge University Press 1974), p.47.
6. H. B. Swete, *The Holy Spirit in the New Testament* (Macmillan & Co. 1909), p.172.
7. R. Webber ("The Concept of Rejoicing in the Letters of Paul", Yale University Dissertation 1970) suggests that Paul is adapting here an epistolary formula of rejoicing. Cf. G. P. Wiles, *op.cit.*, p.53n.
8. J. Denney, *The Epistles to the Thessalonians* (Hodder & Stoughton 1902), p.217.
9. *Ibid.*, p.117.
10. A. S. Peake in EGT iii 500.
11. A. Maclaren in Exp. III ii 107.
12. J. H. Michael, *The Epistle to the Philippians* (Hodder & Stoughton 1928), p.43.

13. J. Moffatt in Exp. VIII viii 474.
14. C. von Weizsäcker, *The Apostolic Age of the Christian Church* (Williams & Norgate 1895), vol.12, p.361.
15. ET IX 7 334-336 (April 1898).
16. *Ibid.*, p.336.
17. G. P. Wiles, *op.cit.*, p.169.
18. GNT 766: "*Summa epistolae: Gaudeo, gaudete.*"
19. Exp. VIII vii 481-493.
20. J. H. Michael, *op.cit.*, p.xif.; also in Exp. VIII xix 49-63.
21. Adapted from JBP.
22. C. K. Barrett, *The Pastoral Epistles* (Clarendon Press 1963), p.44.

CHAPTER 18
(Pages 134—137)

1. A. S. Peake, *Hebrews* (T. & T. Clark n.d.), p.117.
2. See *supra*, p.84.
3. Maeterlinck, as quoted by A. M. Hunter, *Introducing New Testament Theology* (SCM Press 1957), p.116.

CHAPTER 19
(Pages 138—141)

1. Charles Berry as quoted by M. Watcyn-Williams, *The Beatitudes in the Modern World* (SCM Press 1935).
2. F. L. Cross, *First Peter: a Paschal Liturgy* (A. R. Mowbray & Co. 1954), p.14.
3. E. G. Selwyn, *The First Epistle of Peter* (Macmillan & Co. 1946), p.1.
4. C. E. B. Cranfield, *The First Epistle of Peter* (SCM Press 1950), p.24.
5. E. G. Selwyn, *op.cit.*, p.6.

CHAPTER 20
(Pages 142—146)

1. Cf. A. M. Hunter, *Introducing the New Testament*, p.164f.; J. A. Findlay, *The Way, the Truth, the Life* (Hodder & Stoughton 1940).
2. F. T. Palgrave, *The Golden Treasury* (Amalgamated Press Ltd 1905), no.69.
3. J. H. Moulton in A. S. Peake, *A Commentary on the Bible* (T.C. & E.C. Jacks Ltd 1920), p.906.
4. *Ibid.*

CHAPTER 21
(Pages 147—151)

1. Some scholars, while accepting the view that the book in its final form was published in the reign of Domitian, believe that a few passages belong to an earlier date. See T. F. Glasson, *The Revelation of John* (Cambridge University Press 1965), p.13.

2. It is unlikely that the Book of Revelation was written by the same John as the one who wrote the three letters and the fourth gospel. The latter can be referred to as "John the Elder", though for the writing of the gospel he may well have had the help of the Apostle John.
3. My own translation; see Chapter Eight, note 13.
4. J. R. Lowell, "The Present Crisis" in *Poetical Works* (Ward, Lock & Bowden n.d.), p.102f.

CHAPTER 22
(Pages 152—154)

1. Rom.5:11—AV. For a fuller treatment of the "Why?" and the "How?" of Christian joy, see W. G. Morrice, *We Joy in God*.
2. G. G. Findlay, "Joy" in HDB(1) 500.
3. R. E. Backherms, *Religious Joy in General in the New Testament and its Sources in Particular* (Friburg, St Paul's Press 1963), p.10.
4. See the third verse of George Matheson's hymn, "O Love that wilt not let me go".
5. The source of this quotation is unknown.
6. Adamnan, *Life of St. Columba*, Second Preface: "Et inter haec omnibus carus, hilarem semper faciem ostendens sanctam, Spiritus Sancti gaudio intimis laetificabatur praecordiis."
7. R. E. Backherms, *op.cit.*, p.9
8. Nels F. S. Ferré, *God's New Age* (Epworth Press 1964), p.56

INDEX OF AUTHORS AND NAMES

INDEX OF BIBLICAL REFERENCES
(including Apocrypha and Pseudepigrapha)